ISBN 978-0-243-02996-9
PIBN 10784842

English
Français
Deutsche
Italiano
Español
Português

www.forgottenbooks.com

Mythology Photography **Fiction**
Fishing Christianity **Art** Cooking
Essays Buddhism Freemasonry
Medicine **Biology** Music **Ancient
Egypt** Evolution Carpentry Physics
Dance Geology **Mathematics** Fitness
Shakespeare **Folklore** Yoga Marketing
Confidence Immortality Biographies
Poetry **Psychology** Witchcraft
Electronics Chemistry History **Law**
Accounting **Philosophy** Anthropology
Alchemy Drama Quantum Mechanics
Atheism Sexual Health **Ancient History**
Entrepreneurship Languages Sport
Paleontology Needlework Islam
Metaphysics Investment Archaeology
Parenting Statistics Criminology
Motivational

LOVE LETTERS

OR

Letters of Sentiment

WRITTEN BY PERSONS EMINENT IN ENGLISH LITERATURE AND HISTORY

COLLECTED AND EDITED BY

ABBY SAGE RICHARDSON

"Far more than kisses, letters mingle souls,
For thus friends absent meet"

BOSTON

JAMES R. OSGOOD AND COMPANY

1883

12-38065

UNIVERSITY PRESS:

JOHN WILSON AND SON, CAMBRIDGE.

TO

MY LOST FRIEND

𝔍 𝔇𝔢𝔡𝔦𝔠𝔞𝔱𝔢 𝔱𝔥𝔦𝔰 𝔙𝔬𝔩𝔲𝔪𝔢

FILLED WITH UTTERANCES OF HEARTS ONCE WARM AND LIVING,
NOW COLD AND DEAD.

INTRODUCTORY.

It was the fashion often, in days when literature was not so assured and independent a profession as now, to begin a book with a preface addressed to a being, half-shadowy and half-real, who existed in the author's mind as "The Gentle Reader." This reader, in whom the author embodied his public, was entreated graciously to entertain that which had come from the heart of the writer, and to look with sympathy, or at least with criticism animated by kindly interest, on that which was laid before him. It is to this same "Gentle Reader," almost extinct now and not often recalled, — to this shadowy creature between whom and himself the author could fancy there existed a friendly bond, — that this little book is specially commended; indeed, it is to him only that it is offered. The editor can say this with more earnestness because she feels herself in some sense the repository only of those secrets of the heart which are here revealed:

she has only just come from that past in which
these hearts used to beat with passion and tenderness; she feels as if for a time she had found
there the magic alchemy which had recreated them
from their dead ashes; and their utterances have
in them something so personal and so sacred that
now, after having gathered them together from
the obscure nooks and corners of literature where
she found so many of them, she should hesitate to
give them thus openly to any eye but that of the
"Gentle Reader." To him alone, then, are they
given, — these records of passion, of folly, of madness, as well as of loyalty, of devotion, and of
noblest affection, — that under his eyes, beaming
at once with sympathy for human suffering and
charity for human weakness, they may give up
their inmost secrets, and he may read here what
was long since written upon the "red-leaved tab-
lets of the heart," before they fall back again to
dust.

It is claimed by many that this age of ours is
so sordid and practical that any depth of feeling
such as is so frankly expressed in these old letters would awake to-day only wonder or laughter.
If it were necessary to make any plea to the
"Gentle Reader" in favour of sentiment, there
would flock, at such need, a cloud of best and most

triumphant witnesses. But let us hope it is not necessary. If there are no such eloquent letters written now as in the sixteenth century, none so elegant as in the eighteenth, the reason lies perhaps in the fact that steam and lightning have so annihilated distance that expression is disregarded and action takes its place. The lover does not stop to write to his mistress when the steam brings him to her feet; nor the husband pause over the page, writing long messages of tenderness, and assurances of health and safety in absence, when the lightning will take ten words of reassurance to his wife's chamber. So the art of letter-writing has fallen into decay. But let us hope that none of the warmth or tenderness of human hearts is lost in the rapid movement of life. And if we grant that expression grows more reserved, and that the tenderest husband might hesitate to-day to write to his " dearest life " in terms that even the stern Puritan Cromwell found natural and easy, it is not because he feels any less, but because he carries his heart more and more under cover. Let us cherish that hope; because in the most golden age of the world true affection is so rare, and love is a plant of such delicate and beautiful growth.

" *It is a talent to love*," says one of George Eliot's strong-women characters, " *but I lacked it.*"

"The woman who can love, constantly and truly," says Balzac, "is as rare as the great general or the great poet. *One must have the genius to love, and there are few such.*" If this be so, then the records of some of the hearts given here, who have loved and suffered, are all the more touching because they are of the few. To suffer seems, indeed, the fate of most of these hearts who are in earnest in their affection. Whether, after a brief season of happiness, some adverse circumstance comes in, or death divides, or whether (as often happens) offered love is unvalued and wasted, it is certain that in most cases there is something fatal to the long continuance of love's happiness.

It is certain, too, that no person is more undiscriminating than the lover, and that neither virtue nor wit, nor any good quality, is the winning one, where passionate and most prodigal affection is concerned. Quite as often characters scheming, ambitious, selfish, cold-hearted, and quite devoid of tenderness, have won the largest loyalty and devotion. When we read the letters of Mary Wollstonecraft, or poor Otway, or Hester Vanhomrigh, — when we see how such rich souls, passionate and loyal, can wreck themselves upon shallow natures with stony hearts, with neither the talent to love nor the sensibility to value love,

— then we know why the ancient myths made love both cruel and blind.

It is a subtle fact which we discover in studying these old letters, that they reveal not only the writer, whose soul, as Johnson says, " lies naked in his letter," but that, by a sort of refracted light, they show us the soul of the person written to. When we read the passionate outpourings of Keats, and Vanessa, and Otway, the reverent tenderness of Nelson, we see beyond them the shallow and frivolous Fanny, the cold-hearted Swift, the selfish and mercenary Mrs. Barry, the voluptuous and ambitious Lady Hamilton. When we read Lord Peterborough's epistles, we see not only the antique beau who writes the lines, but Lady Howard as well, — the self-contained court beauty, calculating and a little precise, with whom he is playing at love-making. In John Winthrop's letters, Margaret Winthrop, the loyal and submissive Puritan wife, is as clear as in her own writing; and when Dorothy Sidney writes her lord, " *If it be love to think on you sleeping and waking, to discourse on nothing with pleasure but what concerns you, to wish myself every hour with you, and to pray for you with as much devotion as for my own soul, then certainly it may be said I am in love,*" we are as sure that the best blood of the noble line of the Sidneys stirs about that husband's heart when he reads her letter as if we had personally known the man.

It is strange how little the expression of senti_ment varies from century to century. These lines above from Dorothy Sidney might have come from the pen of any loving wife yesterday. Pliny, born in the first century, writing in Rome, begs his wife to write him every day, and tells her he is wretched till she returns, in very much the same phrase as the merchant on 'change wrote his wife to-day, who has just left him for a fortnight's visit. "*My chief happiness is in yours.*" "*Believe, there is nothing I would not do if it would make you happy.*" "*Life is not life now you are away.*" These phrases are never hackneyed in the letters of lovers, and they are found word for word in letters centuries old, or in those of the moment. Love, like Youth, belongs among the immortals; and what he says is forever old, yet forever new.

No one will fancy that this little book claims to contain all the famous love-letters of the past, or that this collection is exhaustive. There is only an attempt to represent different types of affection and different styles of expression. The sentimentality of Sterne contrasts well with the real passion of Farquhar, half-hidden under a laugh; and the affection, tempered with godliness, of John Win-throp is a good foil to the gallant coquetries of Lord Peterborough and the Countess of Suffolk. There are all sorts of guests at this banquet of Love, as in that other symposium, described by Plato, at which the poetic Agathon, the calm Pausanias, the witty Aristophanes, even the hand-some Alcibiades, — a little disordered with wine, yet crowned with violets, — all sat to discourse on Love, each in his own fashion; while above all their varying voices rose that of the great Socra-tes, declaring, "*Love is the desire that good be for-ever present to us. Of necessity, then, love must also be the desire for immortality.*"

NOTE.

THIS little volume bears exactly the same name as a charming comedy by the dramatic author, Mr. BRONSON HOWARD; and I take this opportunity of apologizing to him for what might otherwise seem like an unwarrantable appropriation of a title, and of urging in excuse that this book could not easily have been called anything else than *Old Love-Letters.*

CONTENTS.

———◆———

PART I.

LETTERS OF POETS AND MEN OF LETTERS.

Contents.

———◆———

PART II.

LETTERS OF ROYAL PERSONAGES.

PART III.

LETTERS OF STATESMEN, MILITARY MEN, AND MEN OF AFFAIRS.

Contents.

PART I.

LETTERS OF POETS AND MEN OF LETTERS.

He felt the necessity of being beloved, which no noble mind can be without. — COLERIDGE.

PART I.

LETTERS OF POETS AND MEN OF LETTERS.

Thomas Otway to Mrs. Barry.

THE following letters were written by THOMAS OT-
WAY, the poet, to Mrs. Barry, one of the most popular of
English actresses in the last quarter of the seventeenth
century. Her personation of *Monimia* in *The Orphan*, by
Otway, and of *Belvidera* in his play of *Venice Preserved*,
raised her to the very highest rank in her profession.
"In the gentle passions of Monimia and Belvidera," says
one of her biographers, "she has never been excelled. In
scenes of anger, despair, and resentment she was impetu-
ous and terrible, and yet uttered the lines of sentiment
with a most enchanting harmony."

In spite of her power in depicting the softer passions,
she was neither a tender nor an amiable woman. Tradition shows her as heartless as she was mercenary, with
plenty of admirers, each of whom ministered in some way
to her ambition or her advantage. Otway's imagination
and heart were both at once touched in seeing her act in
the creations of his fancy. She seems to have known how
to keep alive his affection, by an occasional favour, for
seven years. He was a man of sensitive nature and

strong affections; and this hopeless love, joined to other misfortune, drove him to excesses, finally to ruin.

In his last days he was wretchedly poor, and there are varying accounts of the manner of his death, which was miserable enough in any case. One tradition relates that, finding himself without money or friends, he shut himself up in a tavern, resolved to die there; but finally, forced by hunger, he rushed out, and, seeing a gentleman passing, begged for a shilling to buy bread. The man, recognizing in Otway the author of *Venice Preserved*, gave him a guinea. The poet went to the nearest shop and bought bread, and, eating ravenously in the agony of hunger, he was choked to death before he could swallow the first mouthful. He was only thirty-four years old at death.

His mad passion for the heartless object of his love is best painted in his own words.

No date; between 1678–88.

My Tyrant, — I endure too much torment to be silent, and have endured it too long not to make the severest complaint. I love you; I dote on you; my love makes me mad when I am near you, and despair when I am from you. Sure, of all miseries love is to me the most intolerable; it haunts me in my sleep, perplexes me when waking; every melancholy thought makes my fears more powerful, and every delightful one makes my wishes more unruly. In all other uneasy chances of a man's life, there's an immediate recourse to some kind of succour or another: in

want, we apply to our friends; in sickness, to
physicians; but love — the sum, the total of all
misfortunes — must be endured in silence; no
friend so dear to trust with such a secret, nor
remedy in art so powerful to remove its anguish.
Since the first day I saw you I have hardly enjoyed one day of perfect quiet. I loved you early;
and no sooner had I beheld that bewitching face
of yours than I felt in my heart the very foundation of all my peace give way; but when you
became another's, I must confess that I did then
rebel, — had foolish pride enough to promise myself that I would recover my liberty, in spite of my
enslaved nature; I swore against myself I would
not love you; I affected a resentment, stifled my
spirit, and would not let it bend so much as once
to upbraid you. Each day it was my chance to
see or be near you; with stubborn sufferance I
resolved to bear and brave your power, — nay, *did*
it too, often successfully. Generally, with wine
or conversation I diverted or appeased the de-
mon that possessed me; but when at night, returning to my unhappy self, to give my heart an
account why I had done it so unnatural a violence, it was then I always paid a treble interest
for the short moments of ease which I had bor-
rowed; then every treacherous thought rose up,

nor left me till they had thrown me on my bed, and opened those sluices of tears that were to flow till morning. This has been for some years my best condition; nay, time itself, that decays all things else, has but increased and added to my longings. I tell you, and charge you to believe it as you are generous (which sure you must be, for everything except your neglect of me persuades me you are so), even at this time, though other arms have held you, that I love you with that tenderness of spirit, that purity of truth, that sincerity of heart, that I could sacrifice the nearest friends or interests I have on earth barely to please you. If I had all the world, it should be yours; for with it I could but be miscrable, were you not mine.

I appeal to yourself for justice; if through the whole actions of my life I have done any one thing that might not let you see how absolute your authority was over me. Your commands have been sacred to me; your smiles have transported, your frowns awed me. In short, you will quickly become to me the greatest blessing or the greatest curse that ever man was doomed to. I cannot so much as look on you without confusion. You only can, with the healing cordial *love*, assuage and calm my torments. Pity the man, then, that

would be proud to die for you, and cannot live
without you, and allow him thus far to boast that
you never were beloved by a creature that had a
nobler or juster pretence to your heart than the

Unfortunate
OTWAY.

The Same to the Same.

COULD I see you without passion, or be absent
from you without pain, I need not beg your
pardon for thus renewing my vows, that I love
you more than health, or any happiness here or
hereafter. Everything you do is a new charm to
me; and though I have languished for seven long
years, jealously despairing, yet every minute I
see you I still discover something more bewitching.

Consider how I love you. What would I not
renounce or undertake for you? I must have you
mine, or I am miserable; and nothing but knowing
which shall be the happy hour can make the rest
of my life that is to come tolerable. Give me a
word or two of comfort, or resolve never to look
on me more; for I cannot bear a kind look, and
then a cruel repulse. *This minute my heart aches
for you;* and if I cannot have a right in yours, I

wish it would ache till I could complain to you no longer.   Remember poor

OTWAY.

—◆—

Earl of Rochester to Mrs. Barry.

One of Mrs. Barry's lovers, more fortunate than Otway, was the profligate EARL OF ROCHESTER; and the following are two brief notes which he wrote to the actress. It would seem that his brevity was more potent with her than Otway's eloquence; but it must be remembered that Rochester was an earl, and Otway only a poor poet.

MADAM, — Nothing can ever be so dear to me as you are, and I am so convinced of this that I dare undertake to love you as long as I live. Believe all I say, for that is the kindest thing imaginable; and when you can devise any way that will make me appear so to you, instruct me in it, for I need a better understanding than my own to show my love without wrong to it.

—◆—

This is a second letter from the Earl, written at a time when his hand was wounded or disabled.

MADAM, — This is the first service my hand has done me since my being a cripple, and I would not employ it in a lie so soon.   Therefore pray believe me sincere when I assure you that you are very dear to me, and as long as I live I will be kind to you.

P. S. This is all my hand would write, but my heart thinks a great deal more.

———◆———

George Farquhar to Mrs. Oldfield.

GEORGE FARQUHAR was one of the most brilliant writers of comedy during the first decade of the eighteenth century; and Mrs. Oldfield, who played the leading parts in some of his plays, was one of the most charming actresses of that time. When a girl of sixteen or eighteen, she lived with an aunt who kept the Mitre Tavern in St. James's Market, which was the resort of authors, actors, and men of artistic professions. Farquhar, dining there one day, overheard a fresh, musical voice reading aloud with great zest and vivacity a scene from Beaumont and Fletcher's *Scornful Lady.* The reading seasoned his repast, and after it he sought out the reader, and found her young, handsome, and clever. Through his influence, Anne Oldfield became an actress, and was for years one of the queens of the stage.

Farquhar seems to have been seriously in love with her; but, perhaps fortunately for them both, she preferred a richer and more illustrious lover. As for Farquhar, he married a woman who, having lost her heart to him, caused the report to be carried to his ears that a lady of great fortune was dying of an unrequited attachment to

him.   Impelled either by pity or by self-interest, or both
together, he married her to discover that she was as
penniless as himself.   Yet it is told to his credit that he
never reproached her for the deceit about her fortune, but
made her a kind and devoted husband as long as she
lived.

He died poor, and dying left this legacy to his friend
Wilks, the actor, in the following laconic note: —

DEAR BOB, — I have not anything to leave thee to per-
petuate my memory but two helpless girls.   Look upon
them sometimes, and think of him that was to the last
moment of his life, thine.

GEORGE FARQUHAR.

It is not absolutely certain that the following letters are
written to Mrs. Oldfield.   They appear, however, in a collection of his writings in which are "letters to Penelope,"
and this seems to be the name under which he wrote to
the fascinating actress.]

No date.   About 1700.

MADAM, — If I ha'n't begun thrice to write and
as often thrown away my pen, may I never take
it up again.   My head and my heart have been
at cuffs about you these two long hours.   Says
my head, "You're a coxcomb for troubling your
noddle about a lady whose beauty is as much
above your pretensions as your merit is below
her love."

Then answers my heart, "Good Mr. Head,
you're a blockhead; I know Mr. Farquhar's merit

better than you. As for your part, I know you
to be as whimsical as the Devil, and changing
with every new notion that offers; but for my
share, I am fixed, and can stick to my opinion of
a lady's merit forever; and if the fair She can secure an interest in me, Monsieur Head, you may
go whistle."

"Come, come," answered my head, "you, Mr.
Heart, are always leading this gentleman into
some inconvenience or other. Was it not you
that first enticed him to talk to this lady? Your
confounded warmth made him like this lady, and
your busy impertinence has made him write to
her; your leaping and skipping disturbs his sleep
by night and his good-humour by day. In short,
sir, I will hear no more of it. I am *head*, and I
will be obeyed."

"You lie," replied my heart, very angry. "I
am head in matters of love; and if you don't give
your consent, you shall be forced, for I am sure
that in this case all the members will be on my
side. What say you, gentlemen Hands?"

"Oh," say the hands, "we would not forego
the pleasure of pressing a delicious, white, soft
hand for the world."

"Well, what say you, Mr. Tongue?"

"Zounds!" says the linguist, "there is more

ecstasy in speaking three soft words of Mr. Heart's suggesting than whole orations of Seignior Head's. So I am for the lady, and here's honest neighbour Lips will stick to it."

"By the sweet power of kisses, that we will," replied the lips; and thus all the worthy members standing up for the Heart, they laid violent hands (*nemine contradicente*) upon poor Head, and knocked out his brains. So now, Madam, behold me as perfect a lover as any in Christendom, my heart purely dictating every word I say; the little rebel throws itself into your power, and if you don't support it in the cause it has taken up for your sake, think what will be the condition of

The headless and heartless

FARQUHAR.

———◆———

The Same to the Same.

MONDAY, 12 o'clock at night.

GIVE me leave to call you dear Madam, and tell you I am now stepping into bed, and that I speak with as much sincerity as if I were stepping into my grave. Sleep is so great an emblem of death, that my words ought to be as real as if I were sure never to awaken. Then may I never again be blest with the light of the sun and the joys of last Wednesday, if you are not as dear to me as my hopes of waking in health to-morrow morning. Your charms lead me, my inclinations prompt me, and my reason confirms me.

Your faithful and humble servant,

FARQUHAR.

———◆———

The Same to the Same.

WHY should I write to my dearest Penelope when I only trouble her with reading what she won't believe? I have told my passion, my eyes have spoke it, my tongue pronounced it, and my pen declared it; I have sighed it, swore it, and subscribed it. Now my heart is full of you, my head raves of you, and my hand writes to you; but all in vain.

If you think me a dissembler, use me generously like a villain, and discard me forever; but if you will be so just to my passion as to believe it sincere, tell me so and make me happy: 'tis but justice, Madam, to do one or t' other.

Your indisposition last night, when I left you, put me into such disorder that, not finding a coach, I missed my way and never minded where I wandered till I found myself close by *Tyburn*. When blind Love guides, who can forbear going astray? Instead of laughing at myself, I fell to pitying poor Mr. Farquhar, who whilst he roved abroad among your whole sex was never out of his way, and now by a single *She* was led to the gallows. From the thought of hanging I was led to that of matrimony. I considered how many gentlemen have taken a handsome swing to avoid some inward disquiets ; then why should not I hazard the noose to ease me of my torment? Then I considered whether I should send for the ordinary of Newgate, or the parson of St. Anne's ; but, considering myself better prepared for dying in a fair lady's arms than on the three-legged tree, I was the most inclined to a parish priest. Besides, if I died in a fair lady's arms, I should be sure of Christian burial at last, and should have the most beautiful tomb in the universe.

You may imagine, Madam, that these thoughts of mortality were very melancholy, but who could avoid the thought of his own death, when you were sick? And if your health be not dearer to me than my own, may the next news I hear be your death, which would be as great a hell as your life and welfare is a heaven to the most devoted of his sex,

FARQUHAR.

P. S. Pray let me know in a line whether you are better or worse, whether I am honest or a knave, and whether I shall live or die.

Farquhar's Last Letter to Penelope (Mrs. Oldfield?).

Madam, — 'T is a sad misfortune to begin a letter with an *adieu ;* but when my love is crossed, 't is no wonder that my writing should be reversed. I would beg your pardon for the other offences of this nature which I have committed, but that I have so little reason to judge favourably of your mercy ; though I can assure you, Madam, that I shall never excuse myself my own share of the trouble, no more than I can pardon myself the vanity of attempting your charms, so much above the reach of my pretensions, and which are reserved for some more worthy admirer. If there be that man upon earth that can merit your esteem, I pity him, — for an obligation too great for a return must, to any generous soul, be very uneasy, — though I still envy his misery.

May you be as happy, Madam, in the enjoyment of your desires as I am miserable in the disappointment of mine ; and, as the greatest blessing of your life, may the person you most admire love you as sincerely and as passionately as he whom you scorn.

Farquhar.

Alexander Pope to the Misses Blount.

ALEXANDER POPE's friendship for the two sisters, Teresa and Martha Blount, was as famous in its day as the friendship of Walpole for the two Misses Berry, half a century later. Poor, sickly, deformed little Pope was not framed by nature to excite a deeper feeling in his feminine contemporaries than pity, although he seems to have had an ambition to play his part in the gallant love-making of the age. He was so good and devoted a son, that it is sad he could not have had the opportunity to show the same virtues as a husband; and, as one of his latest biographers feelingly says, " The best prescription Pope's spiritual physician could have given, was the love of a good and sensible woman." The nearest approach to such an affection in his life was that between himself and Martha Blount, the younger of these two sisters.

The Blounts were bright, vivacious young women whom Pope had known from boyhood, and who, in 1714, came to live near Pope's villa at Twickenham. At first he seems to have shared his regard about equally between the two, and, as he writes to Teresa, " Even from my infancy I have been in love with one after the other of you." There was, however, on his part, a growing partiality for Martha, and after some jealousy on the part of Teresa, a falling off in his regard for her, which ended in quarrel and estrangement. For the last fifteen years of his life, Martha became his almost constant companion, and at his death he left her the bulk of his fortune. In his last years he was pitifully dependent on her for care and sympathy; and he clung to her affection with most touching helplessness.

He seems to have been desirous that she should separate herself from her family, and lead a more independent life; and the last letter quoted below is one in which he remonstrates with her on her want of independence and resolution in her dealings with her family, who, he elsewhere plainly intimates, were unkind and tyrannical. In his later years he spent the greater part of the time with her, and he speaks of her in a letter to one of his friends, as "a friend — a woman friend! — with whom I have spent three or four hours a day for these last fifteen years."

Pope to Martha Blount.

MAY 25, 1712.

MADAM, — At last I do myself the honour to send you the " Rape of the Lock ;" which has been so long coming out that the lady's charms might have been half decayed while the poet was celebrating them and the printer publishing them. But yourself and your fair sister must needs have been surfeited already with this trifle, and therefore you have no hopes of entertainment but from the rest of this book; wherein (they tell me) are some things that may be dangerous to be looked upon : however, I think you may venture, though you should blush for it; since blushing becomes you the best of any lady in England, and then the most dangerous thing to be looked upon is yourself. Indeed, Madam, not to flatter you, our virtue will be sooner overthrown by one glance of yours than by all the wicked poets can write in an age; as has been too dearly experienced by the wickedest of them all, that is to say, by, Madam,

Your most obedient, etc.

———◆———

Pope to Teresa Blount.

BATH, 1714.

You are to understand, Madam, that my passion for your fair self and sister has been divided with the most wonderful regularity in the world. Even from my infancy I have been in love with one after the other of you, week by week, and my journey to Bath fell out in the three hundred and seventy-sixth week of the reign of my sovereign Lady Sylvia. At the present writing hereof it is the three hundred and eighty-ninth week of the reign of your most serene majesty, in whose service I was listed some weeks before I beheld your sister. This information will account for my writing to either of you hereafter, as either shall happen to be queen-regent at that time.

Pray tell your sister all the good qualities and virtuous inclinations she has, never gave me so much pleasure in her conversation as that one vice of her obstinacy will give me mortification this

month.   Radcliff commands her to the Bath, and
she refuses.   Indeed, if I were in Berkshire, I
should honour her for this obstinacy, and magnify
her no less for disobedience than we do the Bar-
celonians.   But people change with the change
of places (as we see of late), and virtues become
vices when they cease to be for one's interest,
with me, as with others.

Yet let me tell her she will never look so finely
while she is upon earth as she would here in the
water.   It is not here as in most other instances;
for those ladies that would please extremely,
must go out of their own element.   She does not
make half so good a figure on horseback as
Christina, Queen of Sweden; but were she once
seen in the Bath, no man would part with her for
the best mermaid in Christendom.   You know I
have seen you often; I perfectly know how you
look in black and white, I have experienced the
utmost you can do in colours; but all your move-
ments, all your graceful steps, deserve not half
the glory you might here attain of a moving and
easy behaviour in buckram — something between
swimming and walking, free enough and more
modestly half-naked than you can appear anywhere else.   You have conquered enough already
by land; show your ambition and vanquish also
by water.

I could tell you a delightful story of Dr. P., but want room to display it in all its shining circumstances. He had heard it was an excellent cure for love to kiss the aunt of the person beloved, who is generally of years and experience enough to damp the fiercest flame; he tried this course in his passion, and kissed Mrs. E—— at Mr. D——'s, but he says it will not do, and that he loves you as much as ever.

Your, &c.

—◆—

Pope to Martha Blount.

1714.

MOST DIVINE, — It is some proof of my sincerity toward you that I write when I am prepared by drinking to speak truth; and sure a letter after twelve at night must abound with that noble ingredient. That heart must have abundance of flames which is at once warmed by wine and you. Wine awakens and refreshes the lurking passions of the mind, as varnish does the colours that are sunk in a picture, and brings them out in all their natural glowings. My good qualities have been so frozen and locked up in a dull constitution at all my former sober hours, that it is very astonishing to me, now I am drunk, to find so much virtue in me. In these overflowings of my heart I pay you my thanks for those two obliging letters you favoured me with, of the 18th and 24th instant. That which begins with "My charming Mr. Pope," was a delight to me beyond all expression: you have at last entirely gained the conquest over your fair sister. It is true you are not handsome, for you are a woman, and think you are not; but this good-humour and tenderness for me has a charm that cannot be resisted. That face must needs be irresistible which was adorned with smiles, even when it could not see the coronation. I do suppose you will not show this epistle out of vanity, as I doubt not your sister does all I write to her. Indeed, to correspond with Mr. Pope may make any one proud who lives under a dejection of heart in the country. Every one values Mr. Pope, but every one for a different reason: one for his adherence to the Catholic faith, another for his neglect of Popish superstition; one for his grave behaviour, another for his whimsicalness; Mr. Titcomb for his pretty atheistical jests, Mr. Caryll for his moral and Christian sentences; Mrs. Teresa for his reflections on Mrs. Patty, and Mrs. Patty for his reflections on Mrs. Teresa. . . .

Your most faithful admirer, friend,
servant, anything, &c.

The Same to the Same.

CIRENCESTER, no date.

IT is a true saying that misfortunes alone prove one's friendship; they show us not only that of other people for us, but our own for them. We hardly know ourselves any otherwise. I feel my being forced to this Bath journey as a misfortune; and to follow my own welfare, preferably to those I love, is indeed a new thing to me — my health has not usually got the better of my tendernesses and affections. I set out with a heavy heart, wishing I had done this thing the last season, for every day I defer it, the more I am in danger of that accident which I dread the most — my mother's death (especially should it happen while I am away). And another reflection pains me, that I have never, since I knew you, been so long separated from you as I now must be. Methinks we live to be more and more strangers, and every year teaches you to live without me. This absence may, I fear, make my return less welcome and less wanted to you than once it seemed even after but a fortnight. Time ought not in reason to diminish friendship when it confirms the truth of it by experience.

The journey has a good deal disordered me,

notwithstanding my resting-place at Lord Bathurst's. My Lord is too much for me; he walks,
and is in spirits all day long; I rejoice to see him
so. It is a right distinction, that I am happier in
seeing my friends so many degrees above me, be
it in fortune, health, or pleasures, than I can be in
sharing either with them; for in these sort of en-
joyments I cannot keep pace with them any more
than I can walk with a stronger man. I wonder
to find I am a companion for none but old men,
and forget that I am not a young fellow myself.
The worst is that reading and writing, which I
have still the greatest relish for, are growing painful to my eyes. But if I can preserve the good
opinion of one or two friends, to such a degree as
to have their indulgence to my weaknesses, I will
not complain of life; and if I could live to see you
consult your ease and quiet, by becoming independent of those who will never help you to either,
I doubt not of finding the latter part of my life
pleasanter than the former or present. My uneasiness of body I can bear; my chief uneasiness
of mind is in your regard. You have a temper
that would make you *easy* and *beloved* (which is
all the happiness one needs to wish in this world),
and content with moderate things. All your point
is not to lose that temper by sacrificing yourself

to others, out of a mistaken tenderness, which
hurts you and profits not them. And this you
must do soon, or it will be too late; habit will
make it as hard for you to live independent, as
for L—— to live out of a court.

You must excuse me for observing what I think
any defect in you; you grow too indolent, and
give things up too easily, which would be otherwise when you found and felt yourself your own;
spirits would come in as ill-usage went out. While
you live under a kind of perpetual dejection and
oppression, nothing at all belongs to you — not
your own *humour*, nor your own *sense*.

You cannot conceive how much you would find
resolution rise and cheerfulness grow upon you,
if you would once try to live independent for two
or three months. I never think tenderly of you
but this comes across me, and therefore excuse
my repeating it; for whenever I do not, I dissem-
ble half that I think of you. Adieu; pray write,
and be particular about your health.

———◆———

Pope to Lady Mary Wortley Montagu.

Lady MONTAGU is one of the most prominent female
figures in her time, which extends over the first half of the
eighteenth century. We get our first glimpse of her at

eight years of age, set up on the dining-table of the Kit-Kat Club to be toasted as a reigning beauty ; and from that time, till her death, she occupies a large space in the age which alternately admired and traduced her.

She was married at twenty-two to Edward Wortley Montagu, and shortly after her marriage went with her husband on an embassy to Constantinople, whence she wrote some of those letters which contributed to make her famous as a writer. Pope's correspondence with her began during this absence; and after her return from the East she settled near him at Twickenham, and their friendship was flourishing. Even the Blounts were neglected for Lady Mary. Suddenly there was coldness, then an open quarrel, and finally bitter hostilities in which they lampooned each other with a vulgarity rarely to be found except in this elegant "Augustan Age" of literature.

Report says that the cause of the quarrel was the fact that Pope forgot his crooked back and deformed side and the still more important fact that Lady Mary had a husband, and made love to her seriously; and that the lady, instead of repulsing him in earnest, only went into such convulsions of laughter that the vanity of the poet was wounded past cure. Pope was womanish enough to feel all the fury that the poets declare none but a woman wronged can feel, and the quarrels and the lampoons were the consequence. The following was written while Lady Mary was in Constantinople.

MADAM, — If to live in the memory of others have anything desirable in it, it is what you possess with regard to me in the highest sense of the words. There is not a day in which your figure

does not appear before me, your conversation return to my thoughts; and every scene, place, or
occasion, where I have enjoyed them, are as live-
lily painted as an imagination equally warm and
tender can be capable to represent them. Yet how
little accrues to you from all this, when not only
my wishes, but the very expressions of them, can
hardly ever arrive to be known to you? I cannot tell whether you have seen half the letters I
have writ; but if you had, I have not said in them
half of what I designed to say; and you can have
seen but a faint, slight, timorous *échantillon* of
what my spirit suggests, and my hand follows
slowly and imperfectly, indeed unjustly, because
discreetly and reservedly. When you told me
there was no way left for our correspondence but
by merchant ships, I watched ever since for any
that set out, and this is the first I could learn of.
I owe the knowledge of it to Mr. Congreve (whose
letters, with my Lady Rich's, accompany this).
However, I was impatient enough to venture two
from Mr. Methuen's office; if they have miscarried
you have lost nothing but such words and wishes
as I repeat every day in your memory, and for
your welfare. I have had thoughts of causing what
I write for the future to be transcribed, and to
send copies by more ways than one, that one at

least might have a chance to reach you. The letters
themselves would be artless and natural enough to
prove there could be no vanity in this practice, and
to show it proceeded from the belief of their being
welcome to you, — not as they came from me, but
from England.   My eyesight is grown so bad that
I have left off all correspondence except with yourself; in which methinks I am like those people who
abandon and abstract themselves from all that are
about them (with whom they might have business
and intercourse), to employ their addresses only to
invisible and distant beings, whose good offices and
favours cannot reach them in a long time, if at all.
If I hear from you, I look upon it as little less than
a miracle, or extraordinary visitation from another
world ; it is a sort of dream of an agreeable thing,
which subsists no more to me ; but, however, it is
such a dream as exceeds most of the dull realities
of my life.   Indeed, what with ill-health and ill-
fortune, I am grown so stupidly philosophical as
to have no thought about me that deserves the
name of warm or lively, but that which sometimes
awakens me into an imagination that I may yet see
you again.   Compassionate a poet who has lost all
manner of romantic ideas, except a few that hover
about the Bosphorus and Hellespont,—not so much
for the fine sound of their names as to raise up   ·

images of Leander, who was drowned in crossing the sea to kiss the hand of fair Hero. This were a destiny less to be lamented than what we are told of the poor Jew, one of your interpreters, who was beheaded at Belgrade as a spy. I confess such a death would have been a great disappointment to me ; and I believe Jacob Tonson will hardly venture to visit you after this news.

You tell me the pleasure of being nearer the sun has a great effect upon your health and spirits. You have turned my affections so far eastward that I could almost be one of his worshippers ; for I think the sun has more reason to be proud of raising your spirits than of raising all the plants and ripening all the minerals in the earth. It is my opinion a reasonable man might gladly travel three or four thousand leagues to see your nature and your wit in their full perfection. What may we not expect from a creature that went out the most perfect of this part of the world, and is every day improving by the sun in the other. If you do not now write and speak the finest things imaginable, you must be content to be involved in the same imputation with the rest of the East, and be concluded to have abandoned yourself to extreme effeminacy, laziness, and lewdness of life.

I make not the least question but you could give

me great *éclaircissements* upon many passages in Homer, since you have been enlightened by the same sun that inspired the Father of Poetry. You are now glowing under the climate that animated him; you may see his images rising more boldly about you in the very scenes of his story and action; you may lay the immortal work on some broken column of a hero's sepulchre, and read the fall of Troy in the shade of a Trojan ruin. But if, to visit the tomb of so many heroes, you have not the heart to pass over that sea where once a lover perished, you may at least, at ease in your own window, contemplate the fields of Asia in such a dim and remote prospect, as you have of Homer in my translation.

I send you therefore, with this, the third volume of the Iliad, and as many other things as fill a wooden box, directed to Mr. Wortley. Among the rest you have all I am worth, — that is, my works; there are few things in them but what you have already seen, except the epistle of Eloisa to Abelard, in which you will find one passage that I cannot tell whether to wish you should understand or not.

The last I received from your hands was from Peterwaradin; it gave me the joy of thinking you in good health and humor; one or two expressions in it are too generous ever to be forgotten by me. I writ a very melancholy one just before, which was sent to Mr. Stanyan, to be forwarded through Hungary. It would have informed you how meanly I thought of the pleasures of Italy without the qualification of your company, and that mere statues and pictures are not more cold to me than I to them. I have had but four of your letters; I have sent several, and wish I knew how many you have received. For God's sake, Madam, send to me as often as you can; in the dependence that there is no man breathing more constantly or more anxiously mindful of you. Tell me that you are well, tell me that your little son is well, tell me that your very dog (if you have one) is well. Defraud me of no one thing that pleases you, for whatever that is, it will please me better than anything else can do.

I am always yours.

————◆——

This brief note was written to Lady Mary Wortley Montagu after her return from Constantinople, and was one of the last which passed between them.

Pope to Lady Mary Wortley Montagu.

I MIGHT be dead, or you in Yorkshire, for anything that I am the better for your being in town.

I have been sick ever since I saw you last, and have now a swelled face, and very bad. Nothing will do me so much good as the sight of dear Lady Mary. When you come this way, let me see you, for indeed I love you.

————•————

Lady Mary Pierrepont to Edward Wortley Montagu.

The lively Lady MARY WORTLEY MONTAGU, *née* Pierrepont, who had been the object of Pope's passion, was hardly twenty when she met Edward Wortley Montagu. They were married after a rather stormy courtship of two years. Her lover seems to have been rather uncertain in his wooing, and the course of their love was troubled from the outset. "When I foolishly fancied," she writes him, "that you loved me, there is no condition of life I could not have been happy in with you. But I will *never* see you more. If you write, be not displeased if I send it back unopened." And in the very next post she acknowledges a letter from him in such terms as the following.

No date.

I THOUGHT to have returned no answer to your letter, but I find I am not so wise as I thought myself. I cannot forbear fixing my mind a little on that expression, though perhaps the only insincere one in your letter — " I would die to be secure of your heart, though but for a moment." Were this but true, what is there I would not do to secure you?

I will state the case to you as plainly as I can ;
and then ask yourself if you use me well.   I have
showed in every action of my life an esteem for
you that at least challenges a grateful regard.   I
have trusted my reputation in your hands ; I have
made no scruple of giving you, under my own
hand, an assurance of my friendship.   After all
this, I exact nothing from you.   If you find it
inconvenient for your affairs to take so small a
fortune, I desire you to sacrifice nothing to me.
I pretend no tie upon your honour ; but in recompense for so clear and so disinterested a proceeding, must I ever receive injuries and ill-usage?

I have not the usual pride of my sex.   I can
bear being told I am in the wrong, but I must be
told gently.   Perhaps I have been indiscreet: I
came young into the hurry of the world ; a great
innocence and an undesigning gayety may possibly have been construed coquetry and a desire of
being followed, though never meant by me.   I
cannot answer for the observations that may be
made on me.   All who are malicious attack the
careless and defenceless.   I own myself to be
both.   I know not anything I can say more to
show my perfect desire of pleasing you and making you easy, than to proffer to be confined with
you in what manner you please.   Would any

woman but me renounce all the world for one? or
would any man but you be insensible of such a
proof of sincerity?

M. P.

As might have been fancied from this stormy courtship,
in which there does not seem to have been mutual confidence from the beginning, the marriage did not turn out
altogether well. The pair made a runaway match, to escape the opposition of her friends; but very soon after
marriage Lady Mary begins to complain of her husband's
coldness, of the frequency of his absence and the solitude
to which he leaves her. He had frequently predicted during their courtship that their marriage would not prove
happy, and seems to have taken no pains to prove this pre-
diction untrue, while poor Lady Mary, who had all her life
the power of attracting admirers, had not the skill, so much
more rare, of holding the heart of a husband. The following is the letter she sent him on the eve of their elope-
ment.

--------◆--------

The Same to the Same.

FRIDAY NIGHT, August, 1712.

I TREMBLE for what we are doing. Are you
sure you shall love me forever? Shall we never
repent? I fear and I hope. I foresee all that
will happen on this occasion. I shall incense my
family to the highest degree. The generality of
the world will blame my conduct, and the relations and friends of —— will invent a thousand

stories of me.   Yet 't is possible you may recompense everything to me.   In this letter, which I
am fond of, you promise me all I wish.   Since I
writ so far, I received your Friday letter.   I will
be only yours, and I will do what you please.

M. P.

William Congreve to Mrs. Arabella Hunt.

WILLIAM CONGREVE, whose tragedy of the "Mourning
Bride" Dr. Johnson thought contained some lines un-
equalled in English poetry, was contemporary with Farquhar as a dramatist, and was a friend of Pope, Lady
Mary Montagu, Swift, and the other celebrated writers of
this period.

He had several affairs of the heart, the most notable
among them his affection for Henrietta, Duchess of Marlborough, to whom he left at his death most of his fortune.
On her part, the Duchess erected a splendid tomb for him
in Westminster Abbey, and had an effigy of the poet,
dressed as in life, made exactly to resemble him; and this
image (so common report of the time averred), " she ordered
brought to the table when she took her meals, and would
talk to by the hour together."   The force of devotion could
no further go!

There is very little of Congreve's correspondence preserved, and none of his letters to the Duchess of Marlborough.   The following note, which gives very little idea of
the wit and vivacity which flavour his comedies, is written
to Arabella Hunt, a public singer of the time.

WINDSOR; no date.

ANGEL, — There can be no stronger motive to bring me to Epsom, or to the North of Scotland, or to Paradise, than your being in any of those places; for you make every place alike heavenly wherever you are. And I believe if anything could cure me of a natural infirmity, seeing and hearing you would be the surest remedy; at least I should forget that I had anything to complain of, while I had so much more reason to rejoice. I should certainly, had I been at my own disposal, have taken post for Epsom upon receipt of your letter, but I have a nurse here who has dominion over me, a most unmerciful she-ass. Balaam was allowed an angel to his; I'll pray, if that will do any good, for the same grace. I am having great experience in the slowness of that animal; for you must know I am making my journey towards health upon that beast, and find I make such slow advances that I despair of arriving at you or any other blessing till I am capable of using some more expeditious means.

I could tell you of a great inducement to bring you to this place, but I am sworn to secrecy; however, if you were here I would contrive to make you one of the party. I'll expect you, as a good

Christian may everything that he devoutly prays
for.   I am, Madam,

Your everlasting adorer,

W. CONGREVE.

———◆———

Stella and Vanessa.

However JONATHAN SWIFT's biographers may explain
or apologize for him, I have never yet seen a woman who
did not feel for his character both contempt and detesta-
tion. A man who could deliberately and for years outrage
the feelings and lacerate the hearts of two women whose
worst weakness was in the fact that they devotedly loved
him, can be looked at in no amiable light by any woman
with any chivalry for her sex. His sentimental experience
is so interesting that the following letters could hardly be
printed without a prefatory explanation, although the account of Swift's relations with Stella and Vanessa has so
often before been given.

Early in life Swift was secretary in the family of Sir
William Temple, then in the declining years of his states-
manship. Here, at Moor Park, to quote Macaulay's words,
"Swift attended Sir William, as amanuensis, for twenty
pounds a year and his board, dined at the second table,
wrote bad verses in praise of his employer, and made love
to a pretty, dark-eyed girl who waited on Lady Giffard"
(Sir William's sister). This pretty, dark-eyed girl was
Esther Johnson, the "Stella" famous in Swift's correspondence.

When Temple died, Swift, not long after, got his living
at Laracor in Ireland, and went there to enter upon his

duties as clergyman. Stella soon followed him, and took up her abode there. She was accompanied by Mrs. Dingley, a respectable elderly woman, with a small income, and the two lived together in lodgings, not far from Swift. When he went away they moved into his parsonage, vacating it on his return, and going back to their lodgings again.

After Swift's writings had made him famous as "the great Dean Swift," he went more and more frequently to London. He was a power there in the world of literature and affairs, and knew intimately the most distinguished men of his age. Pope, Atterbury, Gay, Congreve, Addison, Peterborough, Bolingbroke, Oxford, all these were his associates. In these absences from home he wrote Stella almost daily, keeping a journal-letter which he despatched regularly, and giving the fullest account of all he said, heard, or did. This is the *Journal to Stella* included in his works, from which extracts are given below. The letters are charming, gossiping love-letters, — charming enough for any man to write, a man even who had a sound, wholesome human heart in his bosom. One can fancy poor Stella gloating over them, extracting the fondness as a bee honey, sleeping with them at night under her pillow, and carrying them about with her by day. But with the tendency to hiding and secrecy, which makes love seem like a crime with this man, Swift never can write out plainly. Not content with calling Esther "Stella," he calls her "M. D." in his letters. He speaks to her in the third person constantly. Although the letters are evidently exclusively hers, he writes in the plural to include Mrs. Dingley; he calls himself "Presto;" and all sorts of hidden allusions veil his letters. One ought to doubt a man who goes so into hiding when nobody seeks.

After some dozen years of this life in Ireland, — years of absolute self-abnegation on Stella's part, — in one of his absences to London Swift met Miss Hester Vanhomrigh, who lived there with her mother and sister, ladies of independent fortune. Swift began visits to them, and a special friendship sprang up between himself and Hester, a cultivated, witty, spirited young woman. To believe (as Swift evidently would have us) that this attractive, clever girl would have given Swift all her heart, and would have behaved as she did all her life after, unless he had at the outset allowed her to suppose that he loved her, and that there was no barrier to his making her his wife, is a belief that outrages probability. At this time one notices that his letters to Stella are less frequent; Stella complains a little of neglect; he does not allude to Miss Vanhomrigh in his letters to Stella except very casually, although he goes almost daily to drink coffee with Miss Hester, whom he calls "Hessy" and "Missessy" and thinks no one ever made such coffee as she. This reserve about mentioning Miss Vanhomrigh to Stella furnishes a fair inference that Miss Vanhomrigh is kept in equal ignorance about "little M. D."

After a year or two of this, Swift, who is as cowardly as he is cold-hearted, begins to be alarmed at the state of affairs. Hester's mother dies, and she resolves to come to Ireland to live. Stella has begun to be jealous. Swift writes to Hester, "If you are in Ireland when I am, I shall see you but seldom. It is not a place for any freedom. . . . I will write you as soon as I can, but I shall always write under cover. If you write me, let some one else direct it." He has already given her the pseudonym of "Vanessa," and he is "Cadenus," or Cad. He is perpetually counselling her to secrecy. When she wishes to write anything special to Cad, she must not use the name, but four dots, thus .... The poor girl writes, "I trust the last letter I wrote you was obscure and constrained enough. *I took pains to write it after your manner, although it would have been much easier for me to have wrote otherwise.*"

Next, from fretting and jealousy, Stella fell seriously ill. It was urged the only thing the Dean could do was to marry her. The only reason he urged against marriage was that he did not mean to marry till he had a certain amount of fortune; but he finally consented on condition the marriage should be kept secret, and in 1716, in the garden of the Deanery, with Mrs. Dingley as witness, he married the woman who for sixteen years or more had devoted her life and soul to him. Some one tells the story of a friend's meeting Swift just after the ceremony, and how the great Dean looked pale and haggard, and rushing past said, " You have just met a most wretched man, but on the subject of his wretchedness you must ask no question." Much time has been spent in guessing what this mysterious cause of Swift's misery was. One would fancy that even to a cold-blooded and cold-hearted man like Swift, the tear-stained face of poor Vanessa looking out for him through the lonely shades of Marley Abbey must have floated beside him like a spectre, as he pronounced his vows to Stella in his sunny garden. One would think he needed no worse cause for wretchedness on his wedding-day than that!

After the marriage, Stella returned to her lodgings, and the Dean to his Deanery, where poor Stella was never admitted to live as his wife to her dying day.

Meantime, for seven years more, the visits to Vanessa continued, although he advises change of air, occupation, visits, evidently as distractions of her affection for him.

She lived at Marley Abbey, near Cellbridge, and her old servant pointed out to a visitor after her death a clump of laurels, trained into a bower, where her writing-table and books were placed, and where, when the Dean came, she used to sit with him. Whenever he came it was her custom to plant a laurel tree to hallow the day, and a clump of these trees marks the place where she used to watch and long for his coming. If, as Boccaccio relates, the basil tree grew green and flourishing from the head of Isabella's murdered lover, surely these laurels drew their freshness and beauty from a woman's heart's-blood.

At the last, worn out by years of such waiting, Vanessa took the fatal step of writing to Stella to ask what relation she bore to Swift. Was she his wife? Stella, who seems gentleness itself, must have been stung by this question. She made no answer to Vanessa, but enclosed the letter to Swift. He took it, and at once set out for Marley Abbey. He entered, found Vanessa, and with one of those awful looks which she says struck her dumb, he threw the crumpled letter before her, and went away. Vanessa never saw him again; and in a few weeks she died — died literally of heart-break. She left directions that her letters and Swift's should be published; but the originals were destroyed. Those that are left are copies; and there are not enough remaining to tell the whole of this sad story.

Swift published the poem of *Cadenus and Vanessa*, which is his account of the affair; and it was much read and admired. Somebody said to Stella, " Dr. Swift writes beautifully about Miss Vanhomrigh," to which she answered, "Oh yes, Dr. Swift could *write beautifully* about a broomstick," — a speech whose little malice even poor Vanessa could forgive, for Stella too had suffered.

Stella outlived her rival five years, and when she was

on her death-bed the great Dean wrote beautiful prayers to read to her; no doubt he read them too, beautifully. But a story (which some of his biographers have discredited) relates that, when at the last she pleaded to be allowed to die under the roof of the Deanery, where she had never lived as his wife, he strode away with one of the black frowns which smote Vanessa's life, and refused even that poor last comfort to the dying woman.

This is the story of Stella and Vanessa which has become almost as famous as the story of Abelard and Heloïse, and which remains still untold to the depths. There is much in this sad episode on which neither these letters nor any written history throws a full light.

Dean Swift to Stella.

London, Sept. 10, 1710.

Here I must begin another letter, on a whole sheet, for fear saucy little M. D. should be angry and think that the paper is too little. I had your letter last night, as I told you just and no more in my last; for this must be taken up in answering yours, saucebox. I believe I told you where I dined to-day; and to-morrow I go out of town for two days to dine with the same company on Sunday. I heard that a gentlewoman from Lady Giffard's house had been at the coffee-house to inquire for me. It was Stella's mother, I suppose. I shall send her a penny-post letter to-morrow, and continue to see her without hazarding seeing my Lady Giffard, which I will not do until she begs my pardon. . . .

Here is such a stir and bustle with this little M. D. of ours; I must be writing every night. I cannot go to bed without a word to them; I cannot put out my candle till I've bid them "good-night." O Lord! O Lord! . . . Well, you have had all my land journey in my second letter, and so much for that. So you've got into Presto's lodgings; very fine truly. We have had a fortnight of the most glorious weather on earth, and still continues. I hope you have made the best of it.

Stella writes like an emperor. I am afraid it hurts your eyes; pray take care of that, pray, Mrs. Stella.

Cannot you do what you will with your own horse? Pray do not let that puppy Parvisol sell him. Patrick is drunk about three times a week, and I bear it, and he has got the better of me; but one of these days I shall positively turn him off into the wide world, when none of you are by to intercede for him. . . .

"Write constantly!" Why, Sirrah, do I not write every day and twice a day to M. D.? Now I have answered all your letter, and the rest must be as it can be. I think this enough for one night; and so farewell till this time to-morrow.

The Same to the Same.

LONDON, October, 1710.

I GOT M. D.'s fourth to-day at the coffee-house. God Almighty bless poor Stella and her eyes and head. What shall we do to cure them, poor dear life? Your disorders are a pull-back for your good qualities. Would to Heaven I were this minute shaving your poor dear head, either here or there. Pray do not write; nor read this letter; nor anything else, and I will write plain for Dingley to read from henceforward, though my pen is apt to ramble when I think who I am writing to. . . . I know it is neither wit nor diversion to tell you every day where I dine; neither do I write it to fill my letter, but I fancy I shall some time or other have the curiosity of seeing some particulars of my life when I was absent from M. D. this time, and so I tell you now. . . . I dined to-day with Mr. Addison and Steele, and a sister of Mr. Addison, who is married to one Mons. Sartre, a Frenchman, prebendary of Westminster, who has a delicious house and garden. Addison's sister is a sort of wit, very like him. I am not fond of her.

I was to-day to see Mr. Congreve, who is almost blind with cataracts growing on his eyes, and his case is he must wait two or three years until the cataracts are riper, and till he is quite blind, and then he must have them couched, and besides he is never rid of the gout, yet he looks young and fresh, and is as cheerful as ever.

. . . I was to-day at Mr. Sterne's lodgings; he was not within, and Mr. Leigh is not come to town, but I will do Mrs. Dingley's errand when I see him. What do I know whether china be dear or no? I once took the fancy of resolving to grow mad for it, but it is now off. I suppose I told you so in some former letter. And so you only want some salad dishes, and plates, and etc.? Yes, yes, you shall; I suppose you have named as much as will cost five pounds.

Now to Stella's little postscript, and I am almost crazed that you vex yourself for not writing. Cannot you dictate to Dingley, and not strain your dear little eyes? I am sure it is the grief of my soul to think you are out of order. Pray be quiet, and if you *will* write, shut your eyes and write just a line, and no more, thus, *How do you do, Mrs. Stella?* That was written with my eyes shut. Faith, I think it is better than when they are open; and then Dingley may stand by, and tell you when you go too high or too low. . . .

I am staying before I can fold up this letter, till that ugly D. is dry in the last line but one. Do not you see it? O Lord, I am loath to leave you, faith, — but it must be so, till next time. Pox take that *D!* I will blot it, to dry it.

[None of Stella's letters to Swift were preserved. The only memento of her found among his effects was a raven tress marked in his hand, "Only a woman's hair."]

—◆—

Hester Vanhomrigh to Dean Swift.

Dublin, 1714.

WELL! now I plainly see how great a regard you have for me. You bid me be easy and you 'd see me as often as you could ; you would better have said as often as you could get the better of your inclination so much, or as often as you re- membered there was such a person in the world. If you continue to treat me as you do, you will not be made uneasy by me long. 'T is impossible to describe what I have suffered since I saw you last. I am sure I could have borne the rack much better than those killing, killing words of yours. Some- times I have resolved to die without seeing you more ; but those resolves, to your misfortune, did not last long, for there is something in human na-

ture that prompts one so to find relief in this world.
I must give way to it, and beg you'd see me and
speak kindly to me ; for I am sure you would not
condemn any one to suffer as I have done could
you but know it.   The reason I write you is because I cannot tell it you should I see you ; for
when I begin to complain, then you are angry,
and there is something in your look so awful that
it strikes me dumb.   Oh that you may but have
so much regard for me left that this complaint
may touch your soul with pity !   I say as little as
ever I can.   Did you but know what I felt, I am
sure it would move you.   Forgive me, and believe
I cannot help telling you this, and live.

———◆———

The Same to the Same.

No date.

Is it possible that you will do the very same
thing I warned you of so lately ?   I believe you
thought I only rallied you when I told you the
other night that I would pester you with letters.
Did not I know you very well I should think you
knew but little of the world, to imagine that a
woman would not keep her word whenever she
promised anything so malicious.   Had not you
better a thousand times throw away one hour at

some time or other of the day than be interrupted
in your business at this rate; for I know 'tis as
impossible for you to burn my letters without reading them as 'tis for me to avoid reproving you
when you behave yourself wrong. Once more I
advise you, if you have any regard for your own
quiet, to alter your behaviour quickly, for I do
assure you I have too much spirit to sit down
contented with this treatment. Because I love
darkness extremely, I here tell you now that I
have determined to try all manner of human arts
to reclaim you, and if all these fail, I am resolved
to have recourse to the black art, which, it is said,
never does. Now see what inconveniences you
will bring both me and yourself into. Pray think
calmly of it. Is it not better to come of yourself
than to be brought by force, and that perhaps at
a time when you have the most agreeable engagement in the world? for when I undertake to do
anything I don't propose to do it by halves. But
there is one thing falls out very luckily for you,
which is, that of all the passions, revenge hurries
me least, so that you have it yet in your power
to turn all this fury into good humour, and depend
on it, and more, I assure you. Come at what time
you please you can never fail of being very well
received.

Dean Swift's Answer to the Above.

IF you write as you do, I shall come the seldomer on purpose to be pleased with your letters, which I never look into without wondering how a brat who cannot read can possibly write so well. You are mistaken. Send me a letter without your hand on the outside and I hold you a crown I shall not read it. But, raillery apart, I think it inconvenient, for a hundred reasons, that I should make your house a sort of constant dwelling-place. I will certainly come as often as I conveniently can; but health and the perpetual run of ill-weather hinders me from going out in the morning, and my afternoons are so taken up, I know now how, that I am in rebellion with a dozen people beside yourself for not seeing them. For the rest you need make use of no black art besides your wits. 'T is a pity your eyes are not black, or I should have said the same of them; but you are a white witch and can do no mischief. If you have employed any of your arts on the black scarf I defy it for one reason. Guess. Adieu, for Dr. P——'s come in to see me.

Hester Vanhomrigh to Dean Swift.

MARLEY ABBEY, CELLBRIDGE, 1720.

BELIEVE me it is with the utmost regret that I now complain to you, because I know your good nature such that you cannot see any human creature miserable without being sensibly touched; yet what can I do? I must either unload my heart, and tell you its griefs, or sink under the inexpressible distress I now suffer by your prodigious neglect of me. 'T is now *ten long weeks* since I saw you, and in all that time I have never received but one letter from you, and a little note with an excuse. Oh, how have you forgot me! You endeavour by severities to drive me from you; nor can I blame you, for with the utmost distress and confusion I behold myself the cause of uneasy reflections to you; yet I cannot comfort you, but here declare that 't is not in the power of time or of accident to lessen the inexpressible passion which I have for . . . .

Put my passion under the utmost restraint, send me as distant from you as the earth will allow, yet you cannot banish those charming ideas which will ever stick by me whilst I have the use of memory. Nor is the love I bear you only seated in my soul, for there is not a single atom of my frame that is not blended with it; therefore don't flatter yourself that separation will ever change my sentiments, for I find myself unquiet in the midst of silence, and my heart at once pierced with sorrow and love. For Heaven's sake, tell me what has caused this prodigious change in you which I have found of late. If you have the least remains of pity for me left, tell me tenderly. No; *don't* tell it, so that it may cause my present death, and don't suffer me to live a life like a languishing death, which is the only life I can lead if you have lost any of your tenderness for me.

———◆———

Dean Swift to Hester Vanhomrigh.

Gallstown, near Kninegad, July 5, 1721.

It was not convenient, hardly possible, to write to you before now, though I had more than ordinary mind to do it, considering the disposition I found you in last, though I hope I left you in a better. I must here beg you to take more care of your health, in company and exercise, or else the spleen will get the better of you, than which there is not a more foolish or troublesome disease, and what you have no pretences in the world to, if all the advantages in life can be any defence against it. Cad assures me he continues to esteem and love and value you above all things, and so will do to the end of his life, but at the same time entreats that you would not make yourself or him unhappy by imaginations. The wisest men in all ages have thought it the best course to seize the minutes as they fly and to make every innocent action an amusement. If you knew how I struggle for a little health, what uneasiness I am at in riding and walking, and refraining from everything agreeable to my taste, you would think it a small thing to take a coach now and then, and converse with fools and impertinents, to avoid spleen and sickness. Without health you will lose all desire of drinking your coffee, and become so low as to have no spirits.

... Pray write me cheerfully without complaints or expostulation, or else Cad shall know it and punish you. What is this world without being as easy in it as prudence and fortune can make it? I find it every day more silly and insignificant, and I conform myself to it for my own ease. I am here as deep employed in other folks' plantations and ditching as if they were my own concern, and think of my absent friends with delight, and hopes of seeing them happy and of being happy with them.

Shall you, who have so much honour and good
sense, act otherwise to make Cad and yourself
miserable? Settle your affairs and quit this scoun-
drel island, and things will be as you desire.

I can say no more, being called away; mais
soyez assurée que jamais personne du monde a été
aimée, honorée, estimée, adorée par votre ami,
que vous. I drank no coffee since I left you, nor
intend to till I see you again; there is none worth
drinking but yours, if myself may be the judge.
Adieu.

———◆———

Lord Peterborough and the Countess of Suffolk.

The correspondence of Lord PETERBOROUGH and HEN-
RIETTA HOWARD, the Countess of Suffolk, is one of the best
examples of that kind of courtly gallantry, fashionable in
the eighteenth century, which amused itself with making
love without much feeling of the passion. It is as pinch-
beck and insincere as the age in which it was written.
But those persons who were playing at love, like Lord
Peterborough, learned how to theorize and reason very
wisely upon what they could not feel; and much of what
they write might be accepted as very gospel in any of
those courts of love held in mediæval times, where the
code of the passion was laid down to lovers as rigidly as a
code in law.

Lord Peterborough was one of the wittiest men of his
time, — for so many years a gallant that he could not put
aside that character, even with age. He must have been
over sixty when this correspondence began.

Although the letters are couched in such high-flown terms, the ancient lover affected to himself and to others to be in dead earnest, and Mrs. Howard seems to have been somewhat embarrassed in what spirit to answer them. She is said to have called upon John Gay, the poet, to help her compose some fitting replies; but Gay, although clever enough at another sort of writing, was much too *naïve* for this kind of retort, and the letters in which Mrs. Howard's feminine pen is plainest visible are by far the best.

Henrietta Howard, the Countess of Suffolk, was one of the court beauties of her century, and for several years a favourite of George II. Later in life she married Sir George Berkeley, and the match turned out a very happy one. After this marriage Lord Peterborough wrote her and her husband very sensibly in the way of friendship.

Horace Walpole, in his gossiping letters, thus describes her: "Lady Suffolk was of a just height, well made, extremely fair, with the finest light brown hair; was remarkably genteel, and always well dressed with taste and simplicity. Those were her personal charms, for her face was regular and agreeable rather than beautiful, and those attractions she retained with little diminution till her death at the age of seventy-nine. Her mental qualifications were not so shining. Her eyes and countenance showed her character, which was grave and mild; her strict love of truth and her accurate memory were always in unison. She was discreet without being reserved, and having no bad qualities and being constant to her connections, she preserved uncommon respect to the end of her life."

A picture of the time shows her as " a tall figure in a green silk with rose-colored ribands, fair hair and skin, a white muslin apron with ruffles, a white round arm, and a

chip hat with flowers, which leaves her light blond hair and
fair broad forehead exposed." It is said that although she
lived to the age of seventy-nine, she was singularly young-
looking always, for she was incapable of the keen feeling
and passionate sorrow which fade the cheek and mark the
brow with lines.

The first of the following letters is that with which Lord
Peterborough opened the correspondence ; then follows one
written after it had fairly opened, with Mrs. Howard's
reply. She was by no means an unpractised letter-writer,
as might be inferred from the fact that she called Gay to
her aid on this occasion, for she exchanged letters with
such men as Dean Swift, Pope, Arbuthnot, Lord Chester-
field, Walpole, and other distinguished men who were her
contemporaries. The letters are not dated, but were probably written between 1720 and 1725.

Lord Peterborough to Henrietta Howard.

As I can as well live without meat or sleep as
without thinking of her who has possession of my
soul, so, to find some relief in never having any
conversation with this adored lady, I have been
forced, when alone, to make many a dialogue
between her and myself; but, alas ! Madam, the
conclusions are all in her favour, and I am often
more cruelly condemned by myself, — nay, more,
her indifference and almost all her rigour are
approved.

Permit me to give you an account of my last
duet with my partner ; and as by the original

articles of our scribbling treaty, you were sincerely to tell me your opinion, so remember your
long silence, and give me an answer to this.

On my part I was representing to her the
violence, the sincerity of my passion; but what I
most insisted on was, that in most circumstances
it was different from that of other men. It is
true I confessed, with common lovers, she was the
person I wished should grant, but with this addition, that she was the only woman that I could
allow to refuse. In a word, I am resolved, nay,
content, to be only hers, though it may be impossible she should ever be mine.

To bear injuries or miseries insensibly were a
vain pretence; not to resent, not to feel, is impossible; but when I dare venture to think she
is unjust or cruel, my revenge falls upon all of
the sex but herself. I hate, detest, and renounce
all other creatures in hoop petticoats, and, by a
strange weakness, can only wish well to her who
has the power and will to make me miserable.

Commonly lovers are animated by the gay
look, the blooming cheeks, and the red lips of the
mistress; but, heavens! what do I feel when I
see anguish and paleness invade that charming
face? My soul is in a mutiny against those
powers that suffer it, and my heart perfectly melts
away in tenderness. But for whom have I such

concern? For that dear lady who scarce thinks of me, or scarce regretteth she makes me wretched.

But alas! it was in this last dialogue I found my misery complete; for you must know, the lady had listened with some attention. Mercy was in her looks, softness in her words, and gentleness in all her air. "Were this all true," she asked, "what could you expect? — what do you think your due?"

Never was poor mortal so dismayed. Though she was absent I had not the courage to make one imaginary request; had she been present I could only have expressed my wishes by one trembling look. Oh, wretched prodigality, where one gives all and dare demand no return! Oh, unfortunate avarice, which covets all and can merit nothing! Oh, cruel ambition, which can be satisfied with nothing less but what no man can deserve!

It was long before I could recover from the terror and amaze into which I had thrown myself. At last I ventured to make this answer: "If what I may pretend to be less than love, surely it is something more than friendship."

The Same to the Same.

LOVE is the general word, but upon many occasions very improperly used; for passions very different, if not quite opposite, go under the same title.

I have found love - in so many disguises and false appearances in others, and even in myself, that I thought the true passion undiscoverable and impossible to be described ; but what I pretend to represent I have so frequently felt, that methinks I should be the better able to express it.

The beginnings of this passion, whether true or false, are pleasing ; but if true, the progress is through mountains and rocks. The unhappy traveller goes through rugged ways, and, what is most cruel, he is walking in the dark on the edge of precipices ; he labours under a thousand difficulties ; — success must cost him dear, and then, alas ! the acquisition is insecure.

The greatest hardship is this : we seem bound to the same port, we sail in treacherous seas in quest of a woman's heart, but without a compass ; there is no beaten path or common road ; as many objects, so many humours ; what prevails with one may displease the other in this fantastic pilgrimage of love ; he that goes out of his way may soonest arrive at his journey's end ; and the bold have better success than the faithful, the foolish than the wise.

But I have undertaken to define this passion

which I allow to be called *love*. It is not the person who could please me most, but her that I am most desirous to please, who is truly adored.

To judge of this let us consider the character of a beauteous female coquette. This creature seems designed to give a man pleasure, and pleasure without pain, though not qualified to give him love ; access is easy, enjoyment sure. Free from restraint or obligations, not fettered with the chains of pretended constancy, you meet her with satisfaction and you part with ease ; and are warm enough for pleasure, not exposed to the heats of jealousy, and safe from the cold of despair. A true epicure (but not a lover) can content himself with this, and this may be agreed to be the pleasure-giving lady.

This is no unlively picture of a woman who can please, but far from that person to whom we resign our hearts in the delicate way of love. How shall I describe the woman capable of inspiring a true, respectful tenderness? Who so fills the soul with herself that she leaves room for no other ideas but those of endeavouring to serve and please her? Self-interest, self-satisfaction, are too natural, too powerful, to be quite destroyed, but they are in a manner laid asleep when at the same time we respect and fear her whom we love.

I must always more or less endeavour to maintain by proof what I assert, but I am not at liberty to pursue a pleasure that may give you too much trouble at a time. I begin my next with telling you what *Amoret* should be, or what I think she is.

——◆——

Mrs. Howard's Reply to the Foregoing.

ONE would imagine, by observing upon the world, that every man thought it necessary to be in love — just as he does to talk — to show his superiority to a brute; but such pretenders have only convinced us that they want that quality they would be thought to have.

How few are there born with souls capable of friendship! then how much fewer must there be capable of love, for love includes friendship and much more besides! That you might mistake love in *others*, I grant you; but I wonder how you could mistake it in *yourself.* I should have thought, if anybody else had said so, he had never been in love.

Those rocks and precipices and those mighty difficulties which you say are to be undergone in the progress of love, can only be meant in the pursuit of a coquette, or where there is no hope of a sincere return. Or perhaps you may suppose all women incapable of being touched with so delicate a passion.

In the voyage of love, you complain of great hardships, narrow seas, and no compass. You still think all women coquettes. He that can use art to subdue a woman is not in love ; for how can you suppose a man capable of acting by reason who has not one of his senses under command? Do you think a lover sees or hears his mistress like standers-by? Whatever her looks may be, or however she talks, he sees nothing but roses and lilies, and hears only an angel.

The civilities of some women seem to me, like those of shop-keepers, to encourage a multitude of customers. Who is so obliging to all her lovers as a coquette? She can express her civilities with the utmost ease and freedom to *all* her admirers alike ; while the person that *loves*, entirely neglects or forgets everybody for the sake of *one*. *To a woman who loves, every man is an impertinent who declares his passion, except the one man she loves.*

Your coquette or " pleasure-giving lady " that can part from you without regret, that cannot feel jealousy, and does not pretend to constancy, I should think a very undesirable thing. I have always imagined that they thought it necessary at least to feign love in order to make themselves agreeable, and that the best dissemblers were the most admired.

Every one that loves thinks his own mistress an Amoret, and therefore ask any lover who and what Amoret is, and he will describe his own mistress as she appears to himself; but the common practice of men of gallantry is to make an Amoret of every lady they write to. And, my lord, after you have summed up all the fine qualities necessary to make an Amoret, I am under some apprehensions you will conclude with a compliment, by saying, *I am she.*

———◆———

Letters of Richard Steele.

DICK STEELE may have had many weaknesses and some vices, but we could forgive a good deal of both to a man who could write so tenderly to a woman as he writes to his "dear Prue." His wife was Miss Mary Scurlock, and the first two of the following letters were written to her during courtship. It is said that she was at first averse to marriage, but surrendered after a month's wooing, and then erased the dates of their letters, that in showing them to a friend it might not appear she was so quickly won.

After marriage Steele's gayety, his conviviality, and his recklessness about getting into debt, must often have made trouble for Mrs. Steele, and she must have had much cause to reproach him. Yet he almost disarms censure by his penitent acknowledgment of his faults and by his constant affection. He is frequently dining out and sleeping out, but he never fails to send Mrs. Steele a loving word before dinner or bedtime.   He goes to dine with Lord Halifax, and writes home : —

I DINE with Halifax, but shall be home at half-after-six.   For thee I die, for thee I languish.

DICK STEELE.

P. S. Dress yourself well, and look beautifully to please your faithful husband.

"All women especially," says Thackeray, "are bound to be grateful to Steele, for he was the first of our writers who seemed both to admire and respect them;" and every woman who reads the last and longest letter quoted here from Steele's correspondence will, I think, feel both gratitude and tenderness.   This was a public letter to be used as a dedicatory epistle to the "Ladies' Library," a work in three volumes, which Steele published in 1714, after they had been seven years married.

Mrs. Steele's correspondence has not been preserved. I find only these few lines of prose and the dozen lines of verse following, to denote in what spirit she met his affection.   The first seems to have been written after a little tiff between the married lovers, probably concerning money matters.

"IT is but an addition to our uneasiness to be at variance with each other.   I beg your pardon if I have offended you.   God forgive you for adding to the sorrow of a heavy heart that is above all sorrow but for your sake."

Mrs. Steele to her Husband.

AH, Dick Steele, that I were sure
Your love, like mine, would still endure;
That time nor absence, which destroys
The cares of lovers and their joys,
May never rob me of that part

Which you have given me of your heart.
Others, unenvied, may possess
Whatever they think happiness;
Grant this, O God, my chief request,—
In his dear arms may I forever rest.

———◆———

Steele to Mary Scurlock.

LORD SUNDERLAND'S OFFICE, 1707.

MADAM, — With what language shall I address
my lovely fair, to acquaint her with the sentiments of a heart she delights to torture? I have
not a minute's quiet out of your sight; and when
I am with you, you use me with so much distance
that I am still in a state of absence, heightened
with a view of the charms which I am denied to
approach. In a word, you must give me either
a fan, a mask, or a glove you have worn, or
I cannot live; otherwise you must expect that
I'll kiss your hand, or, when I next sit by you,
steal your handkerchief. You yourself are too
great a bounty to be received at once; therefore
I must be prepared by degrees, lest the mighty
gift distract me with joy. Dear Mrs. Scurlock, I
am tired with calling you by that name; therefore,
say the day in which you will take that of, Madam,

Your most obedient, most devoted humble servant,

RICH. STEELE.

The Same to the Same.

MADAM, — It is the hardest thing in the world to be in love, and yet attend to business. As for me, all who speak to me find it out, and I must lock myself up, or other people will do it for me.

A gentleman asked me this morning, "What news from Lisbon?" and I answered, "She is exquisitely handsome." Another desired to know when I had been last at Hampton Court. I replied, "It will be on Tuesday come se'nnight." Pr'ythee, allow me at least to kiss your hand before that day, that my mind may be in some composure. O love!

> A thousand torments dwell about thee,
> Yet who would live to live without thee?

Methinks I could write a volume to you; but all the language on earth would fail in saying how much, and with what disinterested passion,

I am ever yours,

RICH. STEELE.

———◆———

Steele to his Wife.

SEPT. 13, 1708.

DEAR PRUE, — I write to you in obedience to what you ordered me, but there are not words to express the tenderness I have for you. Love is too harsh a word for it; but if you knew how my heart aches when you speak an unkind word to me, and springs with joy when you smile upon me, I am sure you would place your glory rather in preserving my happiness, like a good wife, than tormenting me like a peevish beauty. Good Prue, write me word you shall be overjoyed at my return to you, and pity the awkward figure I make when I pretend to resist you, by complying always with the reasonable demands of

Your enamoured husband,

RICH. STEELE.

—◆—

The Same to the Same.

SEPT. 21, 1708.

DEAR, DEAR PRUE, — Your pretty letter, with so much good-nature and kindness, which I received yesterday, is a perfect treasure to me. I am at present very much out of humour upon another account, Tyron having put off payment of my eight hundred, which I ought to have received yesterday, till further time. But I hope when Mr. Clay comes to town to-morrow, he will see me justified. I am, with the tenderest affection,

Ever yours,

5 RICH. STEELE.

The Same to the Same.

SEPT. 30, 1710.

DEAR PRUE, — I am very sleepy and tired, but could not think of closing my eyes till I had told you I am, dearest creature,

Your most affectionate and faithful husband,

RICH. STEELE.

From the press, one in the morning.

——◆——

The Same to the Same.

1714.

DEAR MADAM, — If great obligations received are just motives for addresses of this kind, you have an unquestionable pretension to my acknowledgments who have condescended to give me your very self. I can make no return for so inestimable a favour, but in acknowledging the generosity of the giver. To have either wealth, wit, or beauty is generally a temptation to a woman to put an unreasonable value upon herself; but with all these in a degree which drew upon you the addresses of men of the amplest fortunes, you bestowed yourself where you could have no expectations but from the gratitude of the receiver, though you knew he could exert that gratitude in no other returns but esteem and love. For which must I first thank you, — for what you have denied yourself or what you have bestowed upon me?

I owe to you, that for my sake you have overlooked the prospect of living in pomp and plenty, and I have not been circumspect enough to preserve you from care and sorrow. I will not dwell upon this particular: you are so good a wife that I know you think I rob you of more than I can give, when I say anything in your favour to my own disadvantage. Whoever should see or hear you, would think it were worth leaving all in the world for you; while I, habitually possessed of that happiness, have been throwing away important endeavours for the rest of mankind, to the neglect of her, for whom every other man in his senses would be apt to sacrifice everything else.

I know not by what unreasonable prepossession it is, but methinks there must be something austere to give authority to wisdom, and I cannot account for having only rallied many reasonable sentiments of yours, but that you are too beautiful to appear judicious. One may grow fond, but not wise, from what is said by so lovely a counsellor. Hard fate, that you have been lessened by your perfections, and lost power by your very charms.

That ingenuous spirit in all your behaviour, that familiar grace in your words and actions, has for these seven years only inspired admiration and love.   But experience has taught me, the best counsel I ever have received has been pronounced by the fairest and softest lips, and convinced me that in you I am blessed with a wise friend, as well as a charming mistress.

Your mind shall no longer suffer by your person ; nor shall your eyes for the future dazzle me into a blindness towards your understanding.   I rejoice, in this public manner, to show my esteem for you, and must do you the justice to say that there can be no virtue represented in all this collection for the female world, which I have not known you exert as far as the opportunities of your fortune have given you leave.   Forgive me, that my heart overflows with love and gratitude for daily instances of your prudent economy, the just disposition you make of your little affairs, your cheerfulness in dispatch of them, your prudent forbearance of any reflection that they might have needed less vigilance if you had disposed of your fortune more suitably ; in short, for all the arguments you every day give me of a generous and sincere affection.

It is impossible for me to look back on many

evils and pains which I have suffered since we came together, without a pleasure which is not to be expressed, from the proofs I have had in these circumstances of your unwearied goodness. How often has your tenderness removed pain from my sick head! how often anguish from my afflicted heart! With how skilful patience have I known you comply with the vain projects which pain has suggested, to have an aching limb removed by journeying from one side of the room to another! how often, the next instant, travelled the same ground again, without telling your patient it was to no purpose to change his situation! If there are such beings as guardian angels, thus are they employed. I will no more believe one of them more good in its inclinations, than I can conceive it more charming in form than my wife.

But I offend, and forget what I write to you is to appear in public. You are so great a lover of home that I know it will be irksome to you to go into the world, even in an applause. I will end this without so much as mentioning your little flock, or your own amiable figure at the head of it. That I think them preferable to all other children I know is the effect of passion and instinct; that I believe you the best of wives I know proceeds from experience and reason.

I am, Madam, your most obliged husband and most obedient, humble servant,

RICHARD STEELE.

----◆----

The Letters of Laurence Sterne.

It is difficult to believe that a man so sentimental as LAURENCE STERNE could have been born out of France. He was at every period of his life desperately in love with somebody or other. He says, frankly enough, in apologizing for some one else's weakness, "I myself must ever have some Dulcinea in my heart; it harmonizes the soul."

The first letter quoted below is written to his wife, Miss Lumley, before marriage. She seems to have been as sentimental as himself, and to have held off for several years from marriage with Sterne, who was then a poor clergyman, perhaps fearing he might be less devoted after marriage, as well as from other prudential reasons respecting marriage settlements. She was justified in her hesitation, poor lady, and was, no doubt, a much neglected wife.

One of the affairs which "harmonized" his selfish soul was with Miss Katherine Tourmantelle, a young French lady whom he seems to have known before his marriage, although the letter to her following was written after Miss Lumley became his wife.

But his most remarkable letters were to Mrs. Elizabeth Draper, the wife of a merchant in India, who had come to England for her health, which had suffered from the eastern climate. Their correspondence was published under the title of "Yorick to Eliza." He had introduced himself, in *Tristram Shandy,* as a clergyman by the name of *Yorick,* and retained this soubriquet in his letters. He also had addressed Mrs. Draper as his *Brahmine*, in allusion to her Indian residence, and so called himself her Brahmin. Their correspondence ended when Mrs. Draper returned to India, and the last letter from Sterne is written on her departure.

Sterne's expression of feeling in his *Sentimental Journey*, in his sermons, even in *Tristram Shandy*, impresses me as hollow and insincere. If it had not been for his humour his books never would have become English classics. But his humour, sometimes just flavoured with sentiment, is delicious. It is the Attic salt which preserves his work, and has given such characters as *Uncle Toby* and *Corporal Trim* a place in English literature.

Laurence Sterne to Elizabeth Lumley [*afterwards his Wife*].

No date.

You bid me tell you, my dear L., how I bore your departure for S——, and whether the valley where D'Estella stands retains still its looks, — or if I think the roses or jessamines smell as sweet as when you left it. Alas! everything has lost its relish and look! The hour you left D'Estella, I took to my bed; I was worn out by fevers of all kinds, but most by that fever of the heart with which thou knowest well I have been wasting these two years, and shall continue wasting till you quit S——. The good Miss S——, from the forebodings of the best of hearts, thinking I was ill, insisted upon my going to her. What can be the cause, my dear L., that I never have been able to see the face of this mutual friend but I feel myself rent to pieces? She made me stay an hour with her; and in that short space I burst into tears a dozen different times, and in such affectionate gusts of passion that she was constrained to leave the room, and sympathize in her dressing-room. " I have been weeping for you both," said she, in a tone of the sweetest pity; " for poor L.'s heart, — I have long known it; her anguish is as sharp as yours, her heart as tender, her constancy as great, her virtue as heroic. Heaven brought you not together to be tormented." I could only answer her with a kind look and a heavy sigh, and returned home to your lodgings (which I have hired till your return) to resign myself to misery. Fanny had prepared me a supper, — she is all attention to me, — but I sat over it with tears : a bitter sauce, my L., but I could eat it with no other; for the moment she began to spread my little table, my heart fainted within me. One solitary plate, one knife, one fork, one glass ! I gave a thousand pensive, penetrating looks at the chair thou hast so often graced in those quiet and sentimental repasts, then laid down my knife and fork, and took out my handkerchief and clapped it across my face, and wept like a child. I do so this very moment, my L. ; for, as I take up my pen, my poor pulse quickens, my pale face glows, and the tears are trickling down upon the paper as I trace the word L——. O thou! blessed in thyself and in thy virtues, — blessed to all that know thee, — to me most so, because more do I know of thee than all thy sex. This is the philter, my L., by which thou hast charmed me, and by which thou wilt hold me thine, whilst virtue and faith hold this world together. This, my friend, is the plain and simple magic by which I told Miss—— I have won a place in that heart of thine, on which I depend so satisfied that time, or distance, or change of everything which might alarm the hearts of little men, create no uneasy suspense in mine. Wast thou to stay in S—— these seven years, thy friend, though he would grieve, scorns to doubt, or be doubted; 't is the only exception where security is not the parent of danger.

I told you poor Fanny was all attention to me since your departure, — contrives every day bringing in the name of L. She told me last night (upon giving me some hartshorn) she had observed my illness began the very day of your departure for S—— ; that I had never held up my head, had seldom or scarce ever smiled, had fled from all

society, — that she verily believed I was broken-
hearted, for she had never entered the room, or
passed by the door, but she heard me sigh heavily,
— that I neither eat, nor slept, nor took pleasure
in anything as before. Judge, then, my L., can
the valley look so well, or the roses and jessa-
mine smell so sweet, as heretofore? Ah me! —
but adieu! — the vesper-bell calls me from thee to
my God!

L. Sterne.

—————◆—————

Laurence Sterne to Kitty Tourmantelle.

1759 (?).

My dear Kitty, — I have sent you a pot of
sweetmeats and a pot of honey, neither of them
half so sweet as yourself; but don't be vain upon
this, or presume to grow sour upon this character
of sweetness I give you; for if you do I shall send
you a pot of pickles by way of contraries to sweeten
you up and bring you to yourself again. Whatever changes happen to you, believe me I am
unalterably yours, and, according to your motto,
such a one, my dear Kitty,

" Qui ne changera pas que en mourant."

L. S.

Sterne to Eliza Draper.

These letters have no dates, but were written in March and April, 1767.

I CANNOT rest, Eliza, though I shall call on you at half past twelve, till I know how you do. May thy dear face smile, as thou risest, like the sun of this morning. I was much grieved to hear of your alarming indisposition yesterday; and disappointed, too, at not being let in. Remember, my dear, that a friend has the same right as a physician. The etiquettes of this town (you 'll say) say otherwise. No matter! Delicacy and propriety do not always consist in observing frigid doctrines.

'I am going out to breakfast, but shall be at my lodgings by eleven; when I hope to read a single line under thine own hand, that thou art better, and will be glad to see thy Brahmin.

9 o'clock.

——◆——

The Same to the Same.

I GOT thy letter last night, Eliza, on my return from Lord Bathurst's, where I was heard (as I talked of thee an hour without intermission) with so much pleasure and attention that the good old Lord toasted your health three different times;

and now he is in his eighty-fifth year, says he
hopes -to live long enough to be introduced as a
friend to my fair Indian disciple, and to see her
eclipse all other Nabobesses as much in wealth
as she does already in exterior and (what is far
better) in interior merit. I hope so too. This
nobleman is an old friend of mine. You know he
was always the protector of men of wit and genius ;
and he has had those of the last century, Addison,
Steele, Pope, Swift, Prior, etc., etc., always at
his table. The manner in which his notice began
of me, was as singular as it was polite. He came
up to me one day, as I was at the Princess of
Wales's Court. " I want to know you, Mr. Sterne ;
but it is fit you should know, also, who it is that
wishes this pleasure. You have heard" (continued
he) " of an old Lord Bathurst, of whom your Popes
and Swifts have sung and spoken so much. I have
lived my life with geniuses of that cast, but have
survived them ; and, despairing ever to find their
equals, it is some years since I have closed my
accounts and shut up my books, with thoughts of
never opening them again ; but you have kindled
a desire in me of opening them once more before I
die ; which I now do : so go home and dine with
me ! " This nobleman, I say, is a prodigy ; for at
eighty-five he has all the wit and promptness of a

man of thirty; a disposition to be pleased, and a power to please others beyond whatever I knew; added to which, a man of learning, courtesy, and feeling.

He heard me talk of thee, Eliza, with uncommon satisfaction; for there was only a third person, and of sensibility, with us; and a most sentimental afternoon, till nine o'clock, have we passed! But thou, Eliza, wert the star that conducted and enlivened the discourse; and when I talked not of thee, still didst thou fill my mind, and warmed every thought I uttered; for I am not ashamed to acknowledge I greatly miss thee. Best of all good girls! the sufferings I have sustained the whole night on account of thine, Eliza, are beyond my power of words. Assuredly does Heaven give strength proportioned to the weight he lays upon us! Thou hast been bowed down, my child, with every burden that sorrow of heart and pain of body could inflict upon a poor being; and still thou tellest me thou art beginning to get ease, — thy fever gone, thy sickness, the pain in thy side, vanishing also. May every evil so vanish that thwarts Eliza's happiness, or but awakens thy fears for a moment! Fear nothing, my dear! Hope everything; and the balm of this passion will shed its influence on thy health, and make thee enjoy a spring of youth and cheerfulness, more than thou hast yet tasted.

And so thou hast fixed thy Brahmin's portrait over thy writing-desk, and will consult it in all difficulties. Grateful and good girl! Yorick smiles contentedly over all thou dost; his picture does not do justice to his own complacency.

Thy sweet little plan and distribution of thy time — how worthy of thee! Indeed, Eliza, thou leavest me nothing to direct thee in, — thou leavest me nothing to require, nothing to ask, but a continuation of that conduct which won my esteem and has made me thy friend forever.

May the roses come quick back to thy cheeks and the rubies to thy lips! But trust my declaration, Eliza, that thy husband (if he is the good, feeling man that I wish him) will press thee to him with more honest warmth and affection, and kiss thy pale, poor, dejected face with more transport than he would be able to do in the best bloom of all thy beauty; and so he ought, or I pity him. He must have strange feelings if he knows not the value of such a creature as thou art.

I am glad Miss Light goes with you. She may relieve you from many anxious moments. I am glad your shipmates are friendly beings. You could least dispense with what is contrary to your own nature, which is soft and gentle, Eliza. It would civilize savages; though pity were it thou shouldst be tainted with the office! How canst thou make apologies for thy last letter? 't is most delicious to me, for the very reason you excuse it. Write to me, my child, only such. Let them speak the easy carelessness of a heart that opens itself, anyhow and everyhow, to a man you ought to esteem and trust. Such, Eliza, I write to thee; and so I should ever live with thee, most artlessly, most affectionately, if Providence permitted thy residence in the same section of the globe, for I am all that honor and affection can make me,`

THY BRAHMIN.

The Same to the Same.

MY DEAR ELIZA, — I have been within the verge of the gates of death. I was ill the last time I wrote to you, and apprehensive of what would be the consequence. My fears were but too well founded; for, in ten minutes after I dispatched my letter, this poor, fine-spun frame of Yorick's gave way, and I broke a vessel in my breast and could not stop the loss of blood till four this morning. I have filled all thy India handkerchiefs with it. It came, I think, from my heart. I fell asleep through weakness. At six I woke with the bosom of my shirt steeped in tears. I dreamt I was sitting under the canopy of Indolence, and that thou camest into the room with a shawl in thy hand, and told me my spirit had flown to thee in the Downs, with tidings of my fate; and that you were come to administer what consolation filial affection could bestow, and to receive my parting breath and blessing. With that you folded the shawl about my waist, and, kneeling, supplicated my attention. I awoke, but in what a frame! O my God! "But thou wilt number my tears, and put them all into thy bottle." Dear girl! I see thee; thou art forever present to my fancy, — embracing my feeble knees and raising thy fine eyes to bid me be of comfort; and when I talk to Lydia [1] the words of Esau, as uttered by thee, perpetually ring in my ears: "Bless *me* even also, my father!" Blessing attend thee, thou child of my heart!

My bleeding is quite stopped, and I feel the principle of life strong within me; so be not alarmed, Eliza: I know I shall do well. I have eat my breakfast with hunger; and I write to thee with a pleasure arising from that prophetic im-

---

[1] Lydia was his daughter.

pression in my imagination, that "all will terminate to our heart's content." Comfort thyself
eternally with this persuasion, — "that the best of
Beings (as thou hast sweetly expressed it) could
not, by a combination of accidents, produce such
a chain of events merely to be the source of misery
to the leading person engaged in them." The
observation was very applicable, very good, and
very elegantly expressed. I wish my memory
did justice to the wording of it. Who taught you
the art of writing so sweetly, Eliza? You have
absolutely exalted it to a science. When I am in
want of ready cash, and ill-health will not permit
my genius to exert itself, I shall print your letters
as finished essays, "by an unfortunate Indian
Lady." The style is new, and would almost be
a sufficient recommendation for their selling well,
·without merit; but their natural ease and spirit
is not to be equalled, I believe, in this section of
the globe, nor, I will answer for it, by any of your
countrywomen in yours. I have shown your
letter to Mrs. B——, and to half the literati in
town. You shall not be angry with me for it,
because I meant to do you honour by it. You
cannot imagine how many admirers your epistolary productions have gained you, that have never
viewed your external merits. I only wonder

where thou couldst acquire thy graces, thy goodness, thy accomplishments, — so connected! so educated! Nature has surely studied to make thee her peculiar care, for thou art (and not in my eyes alone) the best and fairest of all her works.

And this is the last letter thou art to receive from me; because the " Earl of Chatham " (I read in the papers) is got to Downs; and the wind, I find, is fair. If so, blessed woman! take my last, last farewell! Cherish the remembrance of me; think how I esteem, nay, how affectionately I love thee, and what a price I set upon thee! Adieu, adieu! and with my adieu let me give thee one straight rule of conduct, that thou hast heard from my lips in a thousand forms; but I concentrate it in one word,

REVERENCE THYSELF.

Adieu, once more, Eliza! May no anguish of heart plant a wrinkle upon thy face till I behold it again! May no doubt or misgivings disturb the serenity of thy mind, or awaken a painful thought about thy children; for they are Yorick's, and Yorick is thy friend forever. Adieu, adieu, adieu!

Samuel Johnson to Mrs. Thrale.

SAMUEL JOHNSON's long friendship with Mrs. Thrale is almost historical. When Mr. and Mrs. Thrale found him one day at his lodgings, in one of his terrible fits of gloom, they generously took him to their pleasant house at Streatham, and for seventeen years their home was quite as welcome to Johnson as if he had owned a share in it. There was always a room set apart for him, a place of honour at table, and Mrs. Thrale, clever and witty, was always ready to pour out unlimited cups of tea and, best of all, to bear with his bursts of ill-temper with the same cheerful spirit with which she seems to have borne everything in life. This friendship continued long after Mr. Thrale's death, and gossip has even whispered that Johnson would have gladly made the vivacious widow his wife if he had not received too decided a repulse.

The friendship continued, however, till it ended in quarrel, which seems to have been no fault of Mrs. Thrale's. It was pretty well known that her first marriage had been one of convenience, with a man almost double her years. She was still a very charming and agreeable woman of about forty, with an independent fortune. It is not strange that she should have felt she had still a right to make a love-match. Perhaps her friends might not have disputed this right as fiercely as they did if her affections had not fallen upon Mr. Piozzi, who was an Italian and a music-teacher residing in London. But on these grounds the marriage was opposed with a bitterness difficult to understand, and Johnson was one of the bitterest of its opponents. Mrs. Thrale, who seems to have felt sincere friendship for the old philosopher, rough and bearish as he was, endeavoured in vain to placate him. He wrote her a most violent remonstrance on the subject, and finally, when he found the marriage an accomplished fact, he sent her the letter — certainly eloquent and touching — which I have quoted third in this series.

The end, however, did not justify his warning, or his comparison of Mrs. Thrale's fate to that of Queen Mary. Mr. Piozzi, who was an amiable, unpretentious man — well connected in his own country, although Johnson contemptuously spoke of him as a "foreign fiddler" — made an excellent husband, and Mrs. Thrale enjoyed twenty-five years of happy wedlock as Mrs. Piozzi, under which name she published all her literary works.

LICHFIELD, Oct. 27, 1777.

DEAREST MADAM, — You talk of writing and writing, as if you had all the writing to yourself. If our correspondence were printed, I am sure posterity — for posterity is always the authors' favourite — would say that I am a good writer too. To sit down so often with nothing to say, — to say something so often, almost without consciousness of saying and without any remembrance of having said, — is a power of which I will not violate my modesty by boasting; but I do not believe everybody has it.

Some, when they write to their friends, are all affection, some are wise and sententious; some strain their powers for efforts of gayety, some write news, and some write secrets: but to make a letter without affection, without wisdom, without gayety, without news, and without a secret, is, doubtless, the great epistolic art.

In a man's letters, you know, Madam, his soul lies naked. His letters are only the mirror of his breast, — whatever passes within him is there shown undisguised in its natural progress ; nothing is inverted, nothing distorted ; you see systems in their elements, you discover actions in their motives.

Of this great truth, sounded by the knowing to the ignorant, and so echoed by the ignorant to the knowing, what evidence have you now before you? Is not my soul laid open before you in these veracious pages? Do you not see me reduced to my first principles? This is the pleasure of corresponding with a friend, where doubt and distrust have no place, and everything is said as it is thought. These are the letters by which souls are united, and by which minds naturally in unison move each other as they are moved themselves. I know, dearest lady, that in the perusal of this — such is the consanguinity of our intellects — you will be touched as I am touched. I have indeed concealed nothing from you, nor do I ever expect to repent of having thus opened my heart. I am, &c.,

SAMUEL JOHNSON.

The Same to the Same.

Written by Johnson to Mrs. Thrale after her friendship for him had begun to decline.

Since you have written to me with the attention and tenderness of ancient times, your letters give me a great part of the pleasure which a life of solitude admits. You will never bestow any share of your good-will on one who deserves better. *Those who have loved longest love best.* A sudden blaze of affection may by a single blast of coldness be extinguished ; but that fondness which length of time has connected with many circumstances and occasions, though it may for a while be depressed by disgust or resentment, with or without a cause, is hourly revived by accidental recollection. To those that have been much together, everything heard and everything seen recalls some pleasure communicated, or some benefit conferred, some petty quarrel or some slight endearment. Esteem of great powers, or amiable qualities newly discovered, may embroider a day or a week, but a friendship of twenty years is interwoven with the texture of life. A friend may be often found and lost, but an *old friend* never can be found, and nature has provided that he cannot *easily* be lost.

The Same to the Same.

After Mrs. Thrale's marriage to Mr. Piozzi was announced, Johnson wrote her the following, — his last letter to her.

LONDON, July 8, 1784.

DEAR MADAM, — What you have done, however I may lament it, I have no pretence to resent, as it has not been injurious to me. I, therefore, breathe out one sigh more of tenderness, perhaps useless, but at least sincere.

I wish that God may grant you every blessing, that you may be happy in this world for its short continuance, and eternally happy in a better state; and whatever I can contribute to your happiness I am very ready to repay for the kindness which soothed twenty years of a life radically wretched.

Do not think slightly of the advice which I now presume to offer. Prevail upon Mr. Piozzi to settle in England; you may live here with more dignity than in Italy, and with more security; your rank will be higher, and your fortune more under your own eye. I desire not to detail my reasons; but every argument of prudence and interest is for England, and only some phantoms of imagination seduce you to Italy.

I am afraid, however, that my counsel is vain, yet I have eased my heart by giving it.

When Queen Mary took the resolution of sheltering herself in England, the Archbishop of St. Andrew's, attempting to dissuade her, attended her on her journey; and when they came to that irremeable stream that separated the two kingdoms, walked by her side into the water, in the middle of which he seized her bridle, and with earnestness proportioned to her own danger and his own affection pressed her to return. The queen went forward. If the parallel reaches thus far, may it go no farther — the tears stand in my eyes.

I am going into Derbyshire, and hope to be followed by your good wishes, for I am, with great affection,   Yours, &c.,

SAMUEL JOHNSON.

———◆———

Letters of Horace Walpole and the Misses Berry.

WALPOLE is well styled the " prince of letter-writers," and he is a most comfortable one to read. One feels as if one were not getting into his confidence clandestinely in reading his letters, they are so evidently intended for any eye, in his own time or later times, which would peruse them with interest. He writes with unflagging vivacity through a lifetime which lasted almost eighty years, and his epistolary production fills nine stout octavos. If one wishes to know all the gossip, fashionable, political, theatrical, literary, and artistic, of the last three quarters of the eighteenth century he can know it as intimately by reading Walpole as if he had taken tea every evening, during that long period, with the most loquacious news-monger of the day.

Walpole was unmarried, and preserved to the last his bachelor estate. But if other gossips than he speak true, he offered himself to each of the Misses Berry in succession

Miss Mary and Miss Agnes Berry were English girls who had been for some years residing in Paris before they came to live in England, near Walpole. He formed for them both a very tender friendship, and one gets a better idea of his heart from his letters to them, than from anything else he ever wrote. They became most valuable adjuncts to his life, and one can fancy his existence would have become dreary without them. He writes to one of his correspondents shortly after meeting them : "I have made a to me precious acquisition. It is the acquaintance of two young ladies of the name of Berry, whom I first saw last winter, and who have taken a house here with their father for the summer."

They finally settled on a small estate of his, sometimes called "Little Strawberry," after his larger house "Strawberry Hill," and he often spoke of the two ladies as his "Strawberries." The small house which they occupied, where beautiful Kitty Clive the actress had once lived, he bequeathed to the sisters in his will.

Although he writes with equal affection to the two sisters, Miss Mary Berry was doubtless the favourite, and the one rumour most frequently assigned to him as a wife. When one of his nieces used to ask him jestingly when she should "call Miss Berry aunt," he answered, "Whenever Miss Berry chooses." Miss Martineau, who met Miss Berry late in life (she lived to extreme age), says she could doubt-less, had she chosen, have been the Countess of Orford.

But if the brilliant old peer ever desired such a marriage his letters rather disavow it, as we shall see in reading some of the following; and his feeling may have been only the tender, half-paternal friendship which a man of seventy-three felt for two sensible and clever young women of twenty-five and six, who were charmed by his wit and knowledge of the world, and ready to cheer his latest years with a great deal of their pleasant society.

———◆———

Walpole to the Misses Berry.

FEB. 2, 1789.

I AM sorry — in the sense of the word before it meant, like a Hebrew word, glad or sorry — that I am engaged this evening; and I am at your command on Tuesday, as it is always my inclination to be.

It is a misfortune that words become so much the current coin of society, that like King William's shillings they have no impression left; they are worn so smooth that they mark no more to whom they first belonged than to whom they do belong, and are not worth even the twelvepence into which they may be changed. But if they mean too little, they may seem to mean too much too; especially when an old man (who is often synonymous for a miser) parts with them. I am afraid of protesting how much I delight in your society, lest I should seem to affect being gallant; but if two negatives make an affirmative, why may not two ridicules compose one piece of sense? and therefore, as I am in love with you both, I trust it is a proof of the good sense of your devoted

H. WALPOLE.

————◆————

The Same to the Same.

Not long after their first acquaintance the Misses Berry went to the Continent for a visit, and it was during this absence that most of Walpole's letters to them were written.

SUNDAY, Oct. 10, 1790.
(The day of your departure for the Continent.)

Is it possible to write to my beloved friends, and refrain from speaking of my grief at losing you, though it is but the continuation of what I have felt ever since I was stunned by your intention of going abroad this autumn? Still I will not tire you with it often. In happy days I smiled and called you my dear wives; now I can only think of you as darling children of whom I am bereaved. As such I have loved and do love you, and, charming as you both are, I have no occasion to remind myself that I am past seventy-three. Your hearts, your understandings, your

virtues, and the cruel injustice of your fate have
interested me in everything that concerns you;
and so far from having occasion to blush for any
unbecoming weakness, I am proud of my affection for you, and very proud of your condescend-
ing to pass so many hours with an old man, when
everybody admires you, and the most insensible
allow that your good sense and information have
formed you to converse with the most intelligent
of our sex as well as your own; and neither can
tax you with airs of pretension or affectation.
Your simplicity and natural ease set off all your
other merits; all these graces are lost to me,
alas! when I have no time to lose.

Sensible as I am to my loss, it will occupy but
part of my thoughts, till I know you safely landed,
and arrived safely in Turin; not till you are there,
and I learn so, will my anxiety subside, and settle
into steady, selfish sorrow.   I looked at every
weathercock as I came along the road to-day and
was happy to see every one pointing northeast.
May they do so to-morrow.

Forgive me for writing nothing to-night but
about you two and myself.   Of what can I have
thought else? I have not spoken to a single person but my own servants since we parted last
night.   I found a message here from Miss Howe

to invite me for this evening. Do you think I have not preferred staying at home to write to you, as this must go to London to-morrow morning to be ready for Tuesday's post?

My future letters shall talk of other things when I know of anything worth repeating, or perhaps any trifle, for I am determined to forbid myself lamentations that would weary you; and the frequency of my letters will prove there is no forgetfulness. If I live to see you again, you will then judge whether I am changed; but a friendship so rational and pure as mine is, and so equal for both, is not likely to have any of the fickleness of youth, when it has none of its other ingredients. It was such a sweet consolation to the short time I may have left, to fall into such society; no wonder, then, that I am unhappy at that consolation being abridged. I pique myself on no philosophy but what a long use and knowledge of the world has given me, — the philosophy of indifference to most persons and events. I do pique myself on not being ridiculous at this very late period of my life; but when there is not a grain of passion in my affection for you two, and when you both have the good sense not to feel displeased at my telling you so (though I hope you would have despised me for the contrary), I am not ashamed to say

your loss is heavy to me ; and that I am only rec-
onciled to it by hoping that a winter in Italy, and
the journeys and sea air will be very beneficial to
two constitutions so delicate as yours.   Adieu,
my dearest friends.   It would be tautology to
subscribe a name to a letter every line of which
would suit no other man in the world but the
writer.

———◆———

    It was after the Misses Berry returned from abroad, that
they took up their abode at "Little Strawberry," which
Walpole had prepared for them.   Innocent and evidently
disinterested as was the friendship of the two ladies for the
old peer, it was made the subject of scandal, even to a
report in the newspaper that they had designs upon his
fortune.   It was to one of these scandalous newspaper
reports that Miss Berry indignantly alludes in a letter to
Walpole from which the following are extracts.

    I DID not like to show you, nor did I feel myself,
while with you, *how* much I was hurt by the newspaper.   To be long honoured by your friendship
and remain unnoticed I knew was impossible and
laid my account with ; but to have it imagined,
implied, or even hinted, that the purest friendship
that ever actuated human bosoms could have any
possible foundation in, or view to, interested motives . . . all this I confess I cannot bear ; not
even your society can make up to me for it.

Would to God we had remained abroad, where we might still have enjoyed as much of your confidence and friendship as ignorance and impertinence seem likely to allow us here. . . . Excuse the manner in which I write and in which I feel. My sentiments on newspapers have long been known to you, with regard to all who have not so honourably distinguished themselves as to feel above such feeble but venomed shafts.

Do not plague yourself by answering this. The only consolation I can have is the knowledge of your sentiments, of which I need no conviction. I am relieved by writing, and shall sleep sounder for having thus unburthened my heart. Good-, night.

———◆———

Miss Berry's letter was answered at once by Walpole in the following.

Dec. 13, 1791.

MY DEAREST ANGEL, — I had two persons talking law to me, and was forced to give an immediate answer, so that I could not even read your note till I had done; and now I do read it, it breaks my heart! If my pure affection has brought grief and mortification on you I shall be the most miserable of men. My nephew's death has brought a load upon me that I have not strength to bear, as I told General Conway this

morning. . . . You know I scarce wish to live, but
to carry you to Cliveden! But I talk of myself
when I should speak to your mind. Is all your
felicity to be in the power of a newspaper? who is
not so? Are your virtue and purity, and my innocence about you, — are our consciences, no shield
against anonymous folly or envy? Would you
only condescend to be my friend if I were a beg-
gar? . . . For your sake, for poor *mine*, combat
such extravagant delicacy, and do not poison the
few last days of life, which you, and *you* only, can
sweeten. I am too exhausted to write more, but
let your heart and your strong understanding remove such chimeras.

How *could* you say you wish you had not
returned?

To Miss MARY BERRY.

———◆———

From that time the friendship continued uninterrupted
till Walpole's death in 1797. There is one slight allusion
to the report of his being in love with them in this letter to
the two ladies written two years after the date of the above.

To the two Misses Berry in Yorkshire.

TUESDAY NIGHT, 8 o'clock, Sept. 17, 1793.

MY BELOVED SPOUSES, — Whom I love better
than Solomon loved his one spouse — or his one

thousand. I lament that the summer is over, not because of its uniquity, but because you two made it so delightful to me that six weeks of gout could not sour it. Pray take care of yourselves, not for your own sakes, but for mine; for as I have just had my quota of gout, I may possibly expect to see another summer; and, as you allow that I do know my own, and when I wish for anything and get it, am entirely satisfied, you may depend upon it I shall be as happy with a third summer, if I reach it, as I have been with the two last.

Consider, that I have been threescore years and ten looking for a society that I perfectly like, and at last there dropped out of the clouds into Lady Herries's room, two young gentlewomen, who I so little thought were sent thither on purpose for me, that when I was told they were the charming Miss Berrys I would not even go to the side of the chamber where they sat. But as Fortune never throws anything at one's head without hitting one, I soon found that the charming Miss Berrys were precisely *ce qu'il me fallait,* and that, though young enough to be my great-granddaughters, and lovely enough to turn the heads of all our youth, and sensible enough, if said youths have any brains, to set all their heads to rights again. Yes, sweet damsels, I have found that you can bear to pass half your time with an antediluvian without discovering any *ennui*, or any disgust, though his greatest merit towards you is, that he is not one of those old fools who fancy they are in love in their dotage. I have no such vagary, though I am not sorry that some folks think I am so absurd, since it frets their selfishness.

I must repeat it, keep in mind that both of you are delicate, and not strong. If you return in better health I shall not repine at your journey. Good-night.

----◆----

Robert Burns to Ellison Begbie.

The affections of BURNS — always inclined to rove — were first seriously fixed on Ellison Begbie, a pretty servant-lass in Lochlie, to whom he wrote the following offer of marriage. Not this letter, however, nor the beautiful verses of *Mary Morrison*, which he addressed to her, had any effect on her heart, and her refusal plunged him for a time into a deep melancholy. Years after he spoke of her as the one among all his early loves who would have made him the most suitable wife.

LOCHLIE, 1780.

MY DEAR E., — I do not remember, in the course of your acquaintance and mine, ever to have heard your opinion on the ordinary way of falling in love, amongst people of our station of life — I do not mean the persons who proceed in the way of bargain, but those whose affection is really placed on the person.

Though I be, as you know very well, but a very awkward lover myself, yet, as I have some opportunities of observing the conduct of others who are much better skilled in the affair of court-ship than I am, I often think it is owing to lucky chance more than to good management that there are not more unhappy marriages than usually are.

It is natural for a young fellow to like the ac-quaintance of the females, and customary for him to keep their company when occasion serves. Some one of them is more agreeable to him than the rest; there is something — he knows not what — pleases him — he knows not how — in her company. This I take to be what is called *love* with the greater part of us; and I must own, my dear E., it is a hard game, such a one as you have to play when you meet with such a lover. You cannot admit but he is sincere; and yet, though you use him ever so favourably, perhaps in a few months, or, at farthest, a year or two, the same unaccountable fancy may make him as distract-edly fond of another, whilst you are quite forgot. I am aware that perhaps the next time I have the pleasure of seeing you you may bid me take my own lesson home, and tell me that the passion I have professed for you is perhaps one of those transient flashes I have been describing; but I hope, my dear E., you will do me the justice to believe me when I assure you that the love I have for you is founded on the sacred principles of virtue and honour; and, by consequence, so long as you continue possessed of those amiable qualities which first inspired my passion for you, so long must I continue to love you. Believe me, my dear, it is love like this alone which can render the married state happy. People may talk of flames and raptures as long as they please, and a warm fancy, with a flow of youthful spirits, may make them feel something like what they describe; but sure am I, the nobler faculties of the mind, with kindred feelings of the heart, can only be the foundation of friendship; and it has always been my opinion that the married life is only *friendship* in a more exalted degree.

If you will be so good as to grant my wishes, and it should please Providence to spare us to the latest periods of life, I can look forward and see that even then, though bent down with wrinkled age, --- even then, when all other worldly circumstances will be indifferent to me, I will regard my E. with the tenderest affection, — and for this plain reason, because she is still possessed of those noble qualities, improved to a much higher degree, which first inspired my affection for her.

> "O happy state, when souls each other draw,
> Where love is liberty, and nature law."

I know, were I to speak in such a style to many a girl who thinks herself possessed of no small share of sense, she would think it ridiculous; but the language of the heart is, my dear E., the only courtship I shall ever use to you.

When I look over what I have written I am sensible it is vastly different from the ordinary style of courtship; but I make no apology. I know your good nature will excuse what your good sense may see amiss.

———◆———

Robert Burns to Mrs. McLehose.

Burns's correspondence with Mrs. McLehose, under the title of "Letters of Sylvander and Clarinda," has been several times published. He met Mrs. McLehose on his second visit to Edinburgh, and a warm affection sprang up between them. But Burns's "marriage lines" to Jean Armour held him in a relation which the law considered binding, and Mrs. McLehose had a husband in the West Indies, who had cruelly left her to a life of poverty and struggle with her children in Edinburgh. Thus there was no hope of marriage between them ; and, after an ardent correspondence, from which the following letters are taken, they separated. Burns returned to Ayrshire and married Jean Armour, who had been turned out of doors by her father while Burns was writing to Clarinda in such rapturous terms in Edinburgh.

Sylvander to Clarinda.

MONDAY EVENING, 11 o'clock, Jan. 14, 1788.

WHY have I not heard from you, Clarinda? To-day I well expected it, and, before supper, when a letter to me was announced, my heart danced with rapture ; but behold, 't was some fool who had taken into his head to turn poet, and make me an offer of the first fruits of his nonsense. "It is not poetry, but prose run mad."

Did I ever repeat to you an epigram I made on a Mr. Elphinston, who has given a translation of *Martial*, a famous Latin poet? The poetry of Elphinston can only equal his prose notes. I was sitting in a merchant's shop of my acquaintance, waiting somebody ; he put *Elphinston* into my hand, and asked my opinion of it ; I begged leave to write it on a blank leaf, which I did, as you shall see on a new page : —

To Mr. Elphinston.

O thou whom poesy abhors !
Whom poesy has turnèd out of doors !
Heard'st thou yon groan ?   Proceed no further !
'T was laurell'd Martial calling murther !

I am determined to see you, if at all possible,
on Saturday evening.   Next week I must sing : —

> " The night is my departing night,
>   The morn 's the day I must awa' :
> There 's neither friend nor foe o' mine
>   But wishes that I were awa' !
> What I hae done for lack o' wit
>   I never, never can reca' ;
> I hope ye 're a' my friends as yet.
>   Gude night, and joy be wi' you a' ! "

If I could see you sooner, I would be so much
the happier ; but I would not purchase the *dearest
gratification* on earth, if it must be at your expense
in worldly censure ; far less, inward peace !

I shall certainly be ashamed of thus scrawling
whole sheets of incoherence.   The only *unity* (a
sad word with poets and critics !) in my ideas is
Clarinda.   There my heart " reigns and revels."

> " What art thou, Love ? whence are those charms,
>   That thus thou bear'st an universal rule ?
> For thee the soldier quits his arms,
>   The king turns slave, the wise man fool.

In vain we chase thee from the field,
   And with vain thoughts resist the yoke:
Next tide of blood, alas! we yield;
   And all those high resolves are broke!"

I like to have quotations ready for every occasion. They give one's ideas so pat, and save the trouble of finding expressions adequate to one's feelings. I think it is one of the greatest pleasures attending a poetic genius, that we can give our woes, cares, joys, loves, &c., an embodied form in verse, which, to me, is ever immediate ease. Goldsmith finely says of his muse: —

"Thou source of all my bliss and all my woe:
Who found me poor at first, and keep'st me so."

My limb has been so well to-day that I have gone up and down stairs often without my staff. To-morrow I hope to walk once again on my own legs to dinner. It is only next street. Adieu!

SYLVANDER.

———◆———

The Same to the Same.

MONDAY, 21st January, 1788.

. . . I AM a discontented ghost, a perturbed spirit. Clarinda, if ever you forget Sylvander may you be happy, but he will be miserable.

Oh, what a fool I am in love! what an extraordinary prodigal of affection! Why are your sex called the tender sex, when I have never met with one who can repay me in passion? They are either not so rich in love as I am, or they are niggards where I am lavish.

O Thou whose I am, and whose are all my ways! Thou seest me here, the hapless wreck of tides and tempests in my own bosom : do Thou direct to Thyself that ardent love for which I have so often sought a return, in vain, from my fellow-creatures! If Thy goodness has yet such a gift in store for me, as an equal return of affection from her who, Thou knowest, is dearer to me than life, do Thou bless and hallow our bond of love and friendship ; watch over us in all our outgoings and incomings, for good ; and may the tie that unites our hearts be strong and indissoluble as the thread of man's immortal life!

I am just going to take your Blackbird, — the sweetest, I am sure, that ever sung, — and prune its wings a little.

SYLVANDER.

—◆—

The Same to the Same.

GLASGOW, February 18, 1788,
Monday Evening, 9 o'clock.

THE attraction of Love, I find, is in an inverse proportion to the attraction of the Newtonian phi-

losophy. In the system of Sir Isaac, the nearer
objects are to one another the stronger is the attractive force : in my system, every milestone that
marked my progress from Clarinda awakened a
keener pang of attachment to her. How do you
feel, my love? is your heart ill at ease? I fear it.
God forbid that these persecutors should harass
that peace which is more precious to me than my
own ! Be assured I shall ever think of you, muse
on you, and, in my hours of devotion, pray for you.
The hour that you are not in all my thoughts —
" be that hour darkness ! let the shadows of death
cover it ! let it not be numbered in the hours of
day ! "

> " When I forget my darling theme,
> Be my tongue mute ! my fancy paint no more !
> And, dead to joy, forget my heart to beat ! "

I have just met with my old friend, the ship-
captain — guess my pleasure ! To meet you could
alone have given me more. My brother William,
too, the young saddler, has come to Glasgow to
meet me ; and here are we three spending the
evening.

I arrived here too late to write by post ; but
I 'll wrap half a dozen sheets of blank paper together, and send it by the Fly, under the name of
a parcel. You shall hear from me next post town.

I would write you a longer letter, but for the present circumstances of my friend.

Adieu, my Clarinda! I am just going to propose your health by way of grace-drink.

SYLVANDER.

———◆———

Burns's Last Letter to Clarinda.

FRIDAY, 9 o'clock, Night,
21st March, 1788.

I AM just now come in, and have read your letter. The first thing I did was to thank the Divine Disposer of events that he has had such happiness in store for me as the connection I have had with you. Life, my Clarinda, is a weary, barren path; and woe be to him or her that ventures on it alone! For me, I have my dearest partner of my soul: Clarinda and I will make out our pilgrimage together. Wherever I am, I shall constantly let her know how I go on, what I observe in the world around me, and what adventures I meet with. Will it please you, my love, to get, every week, or at least every fortnight, a packet, two or three sheets, full of remarks, nonsense, news, rhymes, and old songs?

Will you open, with satisfaction and delight, a letter from a man who loves you, who has loved you, and who will love you to death, through death, and forever? O Clarinda! what do I owe to Heaven for blessing me with such a piece of exalted excellence as you! I call over your idea, as the miser counts over his treasure! Tell me, were you studious to please me last night? I am sure you did it to transport. How rich am I who have such a treasure as you! You know me; you know how to make me happy, and you do it most effectually. God bless you with

"Long life, long youth, long pleasure, and a friend!"

To morrow-night, according to your own direction, I shall watch the window: 't is the star that guides me to Paradise. The great relish to all is — that Honour — that Innocence — that Religion, are the witnesses and guarantees of our happiness. "The Lord God knoweth," and perhaps "Israel, he shall know" my love and your merit. Adieu, Clarinda! I am going to remember you in my prayers.

SYLVANDER.

Mary Wollstonecraft's Letters.

The name of MARY WOLLSTONECRAFT is better known, perhaps, than any exact facts concerning her. That she was the mother of Mary Shelley, the poet's wife, and that she advocated extreme views on Woman's Rights, are the principal facts about her as they exist in the minds of most who have ever heard of her at all. That she was a beautiful and gifted woman, romantic to excess, cruelly wronged in her affections, betrayed where she genuinely trusted, is almost entirely unknown. The story of her life is a most pathetic one. Her childhood and girlhood were blighted by the cruelty and drunkenness of her father, whose brutality at length sent Mary and her two sisters from home, to struggle for a livelihood. To escape from a life too difficult to be borne by a soul less brave than that of Mary Wollstonecraft, one of the sisters married early and most unhappily, and returned upon Mary for support. All the poor girl's early experience of marriage was of the saddest and most revolting sort. To her, woman seemed forced by society to be the prey of man, the victim of brutality and injustice, and she longed, with the natural ardor of her disposition, to see her sex emancipated from what seemed a position of abject slavery. Thus she wrote *A Vindication of the Rights of Woman*, to claim for women superior opportunities for education, and greater social and political rights, — a book embodying ideas then extremely radical, but which, for the most part, are hardly more advanced in sentiment than most of the opinions held by the advocates of Woman's Rights in America or England to-day. This book set her apart as a woman. She was called a radical and an infidel, although in fact she shows in her works and letters a deep and sincere religious feeling.

After she had begun her literary career the French Revolution broke out. She was a natural republican in sentiment, and she sympathized ardently with this revolution, which was to her like the dawn of a new day for France. She went to Paris in '93, and when there found her position, as an Englishwoman, not altogether pleasant

nor safe.   There she met an American, Captain Gilbert
Imlay, whose nationality was a protection to him in those
exciting days in Paris, as it was a sure passport to French
favour to be a citizen of our new republic.   Imlay extended
some courtesy and protection to Mary Wollstonecraft, and
her feeling for him soon became one of the most trusting
affection, — a feeling which he professed to return, and no
doubt did return for a time.   In the condition of things
then existing, it would have been almost impossible for
the pair to have been legally married in France.   And
Mary Wollstonecraft's idea of marriage — generated by the
bitter experience of mother, sister, and friends, in whose
miseries she had shared — was that " a pure and mutual
affection *was* marriage, and if love should die between a
pair who had promised love, the marriage tie ought not
and could not bind."   The story that follows is an old one.
Captain Imlay, whose name no generous mind who reads
the following letters can ever hear mentioned without
execration, took advantage of the ardent and tender heart
which threw itself trustfully into his keeping.   She considered herself his wife until death.   He also addressed
her, both in letters of affection and business, as his
" beloved wife."   But when absence, and other attractions
which came during absence, asserted themselves over the
shallow and base nature of the man, his affection began to
wane.   It is touching to trace the heart of the woman in
these letters, and to see how it asserts itself over all her
theories.   She pours out to him her love, her reproaches,
her fears, in words that seem written in " heart's blood
turned to tears."   It is touching also to read her first vague
consciousness of the distinction between such a love as she
felt and that of which he was only capable.   She writes :
" I have found I have more mind than you in *one* respect ;

because I can, without any violent effort of reason, find food for love in the same object much longer than you can. The way to my senses is through my heart, but, forgive me! I think there is sometimes a shorter cut to yours."

Two or three times they were parted and reunited. The birth of her child drew her more strongly to him, and for her child's sake she strove more ardently to draw him to her. As long as he professed to her that he had no other attachment she clung to him, even when almost hopeless of any affection from him, but at last, finding him engaged in a most unworthy intrigue under the roof which sheltered her and their child, she went out one night, in a state of madness, to put an end to her life. There is nothing outside Hood's *Bridge of Sighs* which can parallel in sadness the description of the poor wretch as she stood on Putney Bridge, in a soaking rain, waiting till her clothes should be so saturated that they would more quickly " drag her down to muddy death." She was rescued, however, by a Thames boatman before life was gone, and was restored to her misery.

One year before her death she married William Godwin, one of the most remarkable men of his time, and died in giving birth to her daughter. For a nature like hers the happiest and most fortunate solution of life's problem is death.

She was buried in St. Pancras Churchyard in London, and it was by this grave, where she was wont to sit and read, and commune with her departed mother, that Shelley sought out Mary Godwin and asked her to become his wife. It was in St. Pancras Church that this congenial pair were afterwards married, as near as possible to the grave of the mother, some of whose finest qualities had descended upon her happier and more fortunate child. Shelley wrote of

Mary Wollstonecraft thus — in the opening of the *Revolt of Islam,* which he dedicates to his wife : —

> " They say that thou wert lovely from thy birth,
>   Of glorious parents, thou aspiring child.
>   I wonder not — for One then left this earth
>   Whose life was like a setting planet mild,
>   Which clothed thee in the radiance undefiled
>   Of its departing glory! Still her fame
>   Shines on thee, through the tempests dark and wild,
>   Which shake these latter days, and thou canst claim
>   The shelter from thy sire of an immortal name."

These letters of Mary Wollstonecraft, which had been returned to her by Imlay, were published after her death by Godwin. He was severely criticised for making them public; and indeed, like the letters of Vanessa to Swift, or of Keats to Fanny Brawne, they are too sacred for the vulgar eye, and ought to be read only by those who have hearts to feel for such suffering and such heart-break as is here made palpable upon the lifeless pages. I have selected a larger number from this collection of letters than usual, because the story they tell is so interesting and so touchingly told. As one letter follows another we see the falling off on the part of the lover, from passion to indifference, to neglect, and probably to dislike of his victim. These poor time-worn letters, tear-stained doubtless, are, like a musical poem of Schumann, — a music full of passionate joy and passionate sadness, — the true story of a " Woman's Life and Love."

Mary Wollstonecraft to Captain Imlay.

PAST 12 o'clock, Monday, August, 1793.

I OBEY an emotion of my heart which made me think of wishing thee, my love, good-night, before I go to rest, with more tenderness than I can to-morrow when writing a hasty line or two under Colonel ——'s eye. You can scarcely imagine with what pleasure I anticipate the day when we are to begin almost to live together; and you would smile to hear how many plans of employment I have in my head now that I am confident my heart has found peace in your bosom. Cherish me with that dignified tenderness which I have only found in you, and your own dear girl will try to keep under a quickness of feeling that has sometimes given you pain. Yes, I will be *good*, that I may deserve to be happy, and whilst you love me, I cannot again fall into that miserable state which renders life a burden almost too heavy to be borne.

But good-night. *God bless you.* Sterne says that is equal to a kiss; yet I would rather give you the kiss into the bargain, glowing with grat-itude to Heaven and affection to you. I like the word *affection* because it signifies something

8

habitual, and we are soon to meet to try whether we have mind enough to keep our hearts warm.

Yours,

MARY WOLLSTONECRAFT.

———◆———

The Same to the Same.

WEDNESDAY MORN, August, 1793.

I WILL never, if I am not entirely cured of quarrelling, begin to encourage " quick-coming fancies" when we are separated. Yesterday, my love, I could not open your letter for some time, and though it was not half so severe as I merited, it threw me into such a fit of trembling as seriously alarmed me. I did not, as you may suppose, care for a little pain on my own account, but all the fears I had had for a few days past returned with fresh force. This morning I am better; will you not be glad to hear it? You perceive that sorrow has almost made a child of me, and that I want to be soothed to peace.

One thing you mistake in my character, and imagine that to be coldness which is just the contrary. For when I am hurt by the person most dear to me, I MUST let out a whole torrent of emotions, or else stifle them altogether, and it appears to me almost a duty to stifle them *when I imagine that I am treated with coldness.* I am afraid that I have vexed you, my own. I know the quickness of your feelings, and let me, in the sincerity of my heart, assure you there is *nothing* I would not suffer to make you happy. My own happiness wholly depends on you, and, knowing you as I do, when my reason is not clouded, I look forward to a rational prospect of as much felicity as the earth affords, with a dash of rapture into the bargain if you will look at me, when we meet again, with the look with which you have sometimes greeted

Your humbled yet most affectionate

Mary.

———◆———

The Same to the Same.

Paris, September, 1793,
Friday Morning.

A man whom a letter from Mr. —— previously announced, called here yesterday for the payment of a draft; and as he seemed disappointed at not finding you at home, I sent him to Mr. ——. I have since seen him, and he tells me he has settled the business.

So much for business. May I venture to talk a little longer about less weighty affairs? How

are you? I have been following you all along
the road this comfortless weather; for when I am
absent from those I love, my imagination is as
lively as if my senses had never been gratified by
their presence — I was going to say caresses;
and why should I not?

I have found that I have more mind than you
in one respect; because I can, without any violent effort of reason, find food for love in the
same object much longer than you can. The way
to my senses is through my heart; but, forgive me!
I think there is sometimes a shorter cut to yours.

With ninety-nine men out of a hundred, a very
sufficient dash of folly is necessary to render a
woman *piquante*, a soft word for desirable; and,
beyond these casual ebullitions of sympathy, few
look for enjoyment by fostering a passion in their
hearts. One reason, in short, why I wish my
whole sex to become wiser is, that the foolish
ones may not, by their pretty folly, rob those
whose sensibility keeps down their vanity, of the
few roses that afford them some solace in the
thorny road of life.

I do not know how I fell into these reflections,
excepting one thought produced it, — that these
continual separations were necessary to warm
your affection. Of late we are always separat-

ing. Crack! crack! and away you go! This joke wears the sallow cast of thought; for, though I began to write cheerfully, some melancholy tears have found their way into my eyes that linger there, whilst a glow of tenderness at my heart whispers that you are one of the best creatures in the world. Pardon, then, the vagaries of a mind that has been almost " crazed by care," as well as " crossed in hapless love," and bear with me a little longer. When we are settled in the country together, more duties will open before me, and my heart, which now, trembling into peace, is agitated by every emotion that awakens the remembrance of old griefs, will learn to rest on yours with that dignity your character, not to mention my own, demands.

Take care of yourself, and write soon to your own girl (you may add dear, if you please), who sincerely loves you, and will try to convince you of it by becoming happier.

MARY.

The Same to the Same.

PARIS, January, 1794,
Monday Night.

I HAVE just received your kind and rational letter, and would fain hide my face, glowing with shame for my folly. I would hide it in your bosom if you would again open it to me, and nestle closely till you bade my fluttering heart be still by saying that you forgave me. With eyes overflowing with tears, and in the humblest attitude, I entreat you. Do not turn from me, for indeed I love you fondly, and have been very wretched since the night I was so cruelly hurt by thinking that you had no confidence in me.

It is time for me to grow more reasonable; a few more of these caprices of sensibility would destroy me. . . .

Write the moment you receive this. I shall count the minutes. But drop not an angry word. I cannot bear it. Yet, if you think I deserve a scolding (it does not admit of a question, I grant), wait till you come back, and then if you are angry one day I shall be sure of seeing you the next.

—— did not write to you, I suppose, because he talked of going to Havre. Hearing that I was ill, he called very kindly on me, not dreaming that it was some words that he incautiously let fall which rendered me so.

God bless you, my love! Do not shut your heart against a return of tenderness; and as I now in fancy cling to you, be more than ever my support. Feel but as affectionate when you read this letter as I did writing it, and you will make happy your

MARY.

———◆———

The Same to the Same.

Written after the birth of their child.

HAVRE, Aug. 19, 1794.

I RECEIVED both your letters to-day. I had reckoned on hearing from you yesterday, therefore was disappointed, though I imputed your silence to the right cause. I intended answering your kind letter immediately, that you might have felt the pleasure it gave me; but —— came in, and some other things interrupted me, so that the fine vapour has evaporated, yet leaving a sweet scent behind. I have only to tell you, what is sufficiently obvious, that the earnest desire I have shown to keep my place, or gain more ground in your heart, is a sure proof how necessary your affection is to my happiness. Still I do not think it false delicacy or foolish pride to wish that your attention to my happiness should arise *as much* from love, which is always rather a selfish passion, as reason, — that is, I want you to promote my felicity by seeking your own. For, whatever pleasure it may give me to discover your generosity of soul, I would not be dependent for your affection on the very quality I most admire. No: there are qualities in your heart which demand my affection; but unless the attachment appears to me clearly mutual, I shall labour only to esteem your character instead of cherishing a tenderness for your person.

I write in a hurry, because the little one, who has been sleeping a long time, begins to call for me. Poor thing! when I am sad I lament that all my affections grow on me, till they become too strong for my peace, though they all afford me snatches of exquisite enjoyment. This for our little girl was at first very reasonable, — more the effect of reason, a sense of duty, than feeling; now she has got into my heart and imagination, and when I walk out without her her little figure is ever dancing before me.

You, too, have somehow clung round my heart. I found I could not eat my dinner in the great room, and when I took up the large knife to carve for myself, tears rushed into my eyes. Do not, however, suppose that I am melancholy, for when you are from me I not only wonder how I can find fault with you, but how I can doubt your affection.

I will not mix any comments on the enclosed (it roused my indignation) with the effusion of tenderness with which I assure you that you are the friend of my bosom and the prop of my heart.

MARY.

———◆———

The Same to the Same.

PARIS, Dec. 26, 1794.

I HAVE been, my love, for some days tormented by fears that I would not allow to assume a form. I had been expecting you daily, and I heard that many vessels had been driven on shore during the late gale. Well, I now see your letter, and find that you are safe; I will not regret, then, that your exertions have hitherto been so unavailing.

   .   .   .   .   .

Be that as it may, return to me when you have arranged the other matters which —— has been crowding on you. I want to be sure that you are safe, and not separated from me by a sea that must be passed. For, feeling that I am happier than I ever was, do you wonder at my sometimes dreading that fate has not done persecuting me? Come to me, my dearest friend, husband, father of my child! All these fond ties glow at my heart at this moment, and dim my eyes. With you an independence is desirable, — and it is always within our reach, if affluence escapes us ; without you the world again appears empty to me. But I am recurring to some of the melancholy thoughts that have flitted across my mind for some days past, and haunted my dreams.

My little darling is indeed a sweet child ; and I am sorry that you are not here to see her little mind unfold itself. You talk of " dalliance," but certainly no lover was ever more attached to his mistress than she is to me. Her eyes follow me everywhere, and by affection I have the most despotic power over her. She is all vivacity or softness — yes, I love her more than I thought I should. When I have been hurt at your stay, I have embraced her as my only comfort — when pleased with you — for looking and laughing like you ; nay, I cannot, I find, long be angry with you, whilst I am kissing her for resembling you. But there would be no end to these details. Fold us both to your heart ; for I am truly and affectionately

Yours,　　　　MARY.

The Same to the Same.

PARIS, Dec. 30, 1794.

SHOULD you receive three or four of the letters at once, which I have written lately, do not think

of Sir John Brute, for I do not mean to wife you.
I only take advantage of every occasion, that one
out of three of my epistles may reach your hands,
and inform you that I am not of ——'s opinion,
who talks till he makes me angry, of the necessity
of your staying two or three months longer. I
do not like this life of continual inquietude, and,
entre nous, I am determined to try to earn some
money here myself, in order to convince you that,
if you choose to run about the world to get a fortune, it is for yourself; for the little girl and I
will live without your assistance unless you are
with us. I may be termed proud; be it so, but
I will never abandon certain principles of action.

The common run of men have such an ignoble
way of thinking, that, if they debauch their hearts
and prostitute their persons, following perhaps
a gust of inebriation, they suppose the wife —
slave, rather — whom they maintain, has no right
to complain, and ought to receive the sultan,
whenever he deigns to return, with open arms,
though his have been polluted by half a hundred
promiscuous amours during his absence.

I consider fidelity and constancy as two dis-
tinct things, yet the former is necessary to give
life to the other; and such a degree of respect do
I think due to myself, that, if only probity, which

is a good thing in its place, brings you back, never return, — for if a wandering of the heart or even a caprice of the imagination detains you, there is an end of all my hopes of happiness. I could not forgive it if I would.

I have gotten into a melancholy mood, you perceive. You know my opinion of men in general; you know I think them systematic tyrants, and that it is the rarest thing in the world to meet with a man with sufficient delicacy of feeling to govern desire. When I am thus sad I lament that my little darling, fondly as I dote on her, is a girl. I am sorry to have a tie to a world that for me is ever sown with thorns.

You will call this an ill-humoured letter, when, in fact, it is the strongest proof of affection I can give, to dread to lose you. —— has taken such pains to convince me that you must and ought to stay, that it has inconceivably depressed my spirits. You have always known my opinion. I have ever declared that two people who mean to live together ought not to be long separated. If certain things are more necessary to you than to me, search for them. Say but one word, and you shall never hear of me more. If not, for God's sake, let us struggle with poverty, — with any evil but these continual inquietudes of business, which

I have been told were to last but a few months, though every day the end appears more distant. This is the first letter in this strain that I have determined to forward to you; the rest lie by, because I was unwilling to give you pain; and I should not now write if I did not think that there would be no conclusion to your schemes, which demand, as I am told, your presence.

The Same to the Same.

PARIS, Feb. 9, 1795.

THE melancholy presentiment has for some time hung on my spirits, that we are parted forever; and the letters I received this day by Mr. —— convince me that it was not without foundation. You allude to some other letters, which I suppose have miscarried; for most of those I have got were only a few hasty lines, calculated to wound the tenderness the sight of the superscription excited.

I mean not, however, to complain; yet so many feelings are struggling for utterance, and agitating a heart almost bursting with anguish, that I find it very difficult to write with any degree of coherence.

You left me indisposed, though you have taken no notice of it; and the most fatiguing journey I ever had contributed to continue it. However,

I recovered my health; but a neglected cold and continual inquietude during the last two months have reduced me to a state of weakness I never before experienced. Those who did not know that the canker-worm was at work at the core, cautioned me about suckling my child too long. God preserve this poor child, and render her happier than her mother!

But I am wandering from my subject; indeed my head turns giddy when I think that all the confidence I have had in the affection of others is come to this. I have done my duty to you and my child; and if I am not to have any return of affection to reward me, I have the sad consolation of knowing that I have deserved a better fate. My soul is weary, I am sick at heart; and, but for this little darling, I would cease to care about a life which is now stripped of every charm.

You see how stupid I am, uttering declamation when I meant simply to tell you that I consider your requesting me to come to you as merely dictated by honour. Indeed, I scarcely understand you. You request me to come, and then tell me that you have not given up all thoughts of returning to this place.

When I determined to live with you, I was only governed by affection. I would share poverty with you, but I turn with affright from the sea of trouble on which you are entering. I have certain principles of action; I know what I look for to found my happiness on. It is not money. With you I wished for sufficient to procure the comforts of life; as it is, less will do. I can still exert myself to obtain the necessaries of life for my child, and she does not want more at present. I have two or three plans in my head to earn our subsistence; for do not suppose that, neglected by you, I will lie under obligations of a pecuniary kind to you. No; I would sooner submit to menial service. I wanted the support of your affection; that gone, all is over. I did not think, when I complained of ——'s contemptible avidity to accumulate money, that he would have dragged you into his schemes.

I cannot write. I enclose a fragment of a letter written soon after your departure, and another which tenderness made me keep back when it was written. You will see there the sentiments of a calmer, though not a more determined moment. Do not insult me by saying that " our being together is paramount to every other consideration." Were it, you would not be running after a bubble, at the expense of my peace of mind.

Perhaps this is the last letter you will ever receive from me.

The Same to the Same.

In the course of their correspondence Mary Wollstone-craft went to Sweden, whence she wrote a collection of letters, which are published, among her other works, under the title of *Letters from Norway, Sweden, and Denmark.*

SWEDEN, July 3, 1795.

THERE was a gloominess diffused through your last letter, the impression of which still rests on my mind; though, recollecting how quickly you throw off the forcible feelings of the moment, I flatter myself it has long since given place to your usual cheerfulness.

Believe me (and my eyes fill with tears of tenderness as I assure you), there is nothing I would not endure in the way of privation rather than disturb your tranquillity. If I am fated to be unhappy, I will labour to hide my sorrows in my own bosom, and you shall always find me a faithful, affectionate friend.

I grow more and more attached to my little girl, and I cherish this affection without fear, because it must be a long time before it can become bitterness of soul. She is an interesting creature. On shipboard, how often, as I gazed at the sea, have I longed to bury my troubled bosom in its less troubled deep, — asserting, with Brutus, "that the virtue I had followed too far was merely an empty name;" and nothing but the sight of her — her playful smiles, which seemed to cling and twine round my heart — could have stopped me.

What peculiar misery has fallen to my share! To act up to my principles, I have laid the strictest restraint on my very thoughts. Yes; not to sully the delicacy of my feelings, I have reined in my imagination, and started with affright from every sensation that, stealing with balmy sweetness into my soul, led me to scent from afar the fragrance of reviving nature.

My friend, I have paid dearly for one conviction. Love, in some minds, is an affair of sentiment, arising from the same delicacy of perception (or taste) as renders them alive to the beauties of nature, poetry, &c., — alive to the charms of those evanescent graces that are, as it were, impalpable; they must be felt, they cannot be described.

Love is a want of the heart. I have examined myself lately with more care than formerly, and find that to deaden is not to calm the mind. Aiming at tranquillity, I have almost destroyed all the energy of my soul, — almost rooted out

what renders it estimable.   Yes, I have damped
that enthusiasm of character which converts the
grossest materials into a fuel that imperceptibly
feeds hopes which aspire above common enjoyment.   Despair, since the birth of my child, has
rendered me stupid ; soul and body seem fading
away before the withering touch of disappointment.

I am now endeavouring to recover myself; and
such is the elasticity of my constitution and the
purity of the atmosphere here, that health un-
sought for begins to reanimate my countenance·
I have the sincerest esteem and affection for you ;
but the desire of regaining peace (do you understand me?) has made me forget the respect due to
my own emotions, — sacred emotions that are the
sure harbingers of the delights I was formed to
enjoy, and shall enjoy ; for nothing can extinguish
the heavenly spark.

Still, when we meet again I will not torment
you, I promise you.   I blush when I recollect
my former conduct, and will not in future con-
found myself with the beings whom I feel to
be my inferiors.   I will listen to delicacy or
pride.

The Same to the Same.

Sweden, July 4, 1795.

I HOPE to hear from you by to-morrow's mail. My dearest friend! I cannot tear my affections from you; and though every remembrance stings me to my very soul, I think of you till I make allowance for the very defects of character that have given such a cruel stab to my peace.

Still, however, I am more alive than you have seen me for a long, long time. I have a degree of vivacity, even in my grief, which is preferable to the benumbing stupor that, for the last year, has frozen up all my faculties. Perhaps this change is more owing to returning health than to the vigour of my reason; for, in spite of sadness (and surely I have had my share), the purity of this air, and the being continually out in it, — for I sleep in the country every night, — has made an alteration in my appearance that really surprises me. The rosy fingers of health already streak my cheeks, and I have seen a *physical* life in my eyes, after I have been climbing the rocks, that resembled the fond, credulous hopes of youth.

With what a cruel sigh have I recollected that I had forgotten to hope! Reason, or rather experience, does not thus cruelly damp poor

Fanny's pleasures; she plays all day in the garden with ——'s children, and makes friends for
herself.

Do not tell me that you are happier without
us. Will you not come to us in Switzerland?
Ah, why do not you love us with more sentiment?
Why are you a creature of such sympathy that
the warmth of your feelings, or rather the quickness of your senses, hardens your heart? It is
my misfortune that my imagination is perpetually
shading your defects and lending you charms,
whilst the grossness of your senses makes you
(call me not vain) overlook graces in me that only
dignity of mind and the sensibility of an expanded
heart can give. God bless you! Adieu.

——◆——

The Same to the Same.

TONSBERG, July 30, 1795.

I HAVE just received two of your letters, dated
the 26th and 30th of June, and you must have
received several from me, informing you of my
detention and how much I was hurt by your
silence.

.   .   .   .   .

Write to me then, my friend, and write explic-
itly. I have suffered, God knows, since I left you.

Ah, you have never felt this kind of sickness of heart! My mind, however, is at present painfully active, and the sympathy I feel almost rises to agony. But this is not a subject of complaint; it has afforded me pleasure, — and reflected pleasure is all I have to hope for, if a spark of hope be yet alive in my forlorn bosom.

I will try to write with a degree of composure. I wish for us to live together because I want you to acquire an habitual tenderness for my poor girl. I cannot bear to think of leaving her alone in the world, or that she should only be protected by your sense of duty. Next to preserving her, my most earnest wish is not to disturb your peace. I have nothing to expect, and little to fear, in life. There are wounds that can never be healed; but they may be allowed to fester in silence without wincing.

When we meet again you shall be convinced that I have more resolution than you give me credit for. I will not torment you. If I am destined always to be disappointed and unhappy, I will conceal the anguish I cannot dissipate; and the tightened cord of life or reason will at last snap, and set me free.

Yes; I shall be happy. This heart is worthy of the bliss its feelings anticipate; and I cannot even persuade myself, wretched as they have made me, that my principles and sentiments are not founded in nature and truth.   But to have done with these subjects.

.   .   .   .   .

I have been seriously employed in this way since I came to Tonsberg; yet I never was so much in the air.   I walk, I ride on horseback, row, bathe, and even sleep in the fields; my health is consequently improved.   The child, Marguerite informs me, is well.   I long to be with her.

Write to me immediately.   Were I only to think of myself, I could wish you to return to me poor, with the simplicity of character, part of which you seem lately to have lost, that first attached me to you.

Yours most affectionately,

MARY IMLAY.

—◆—

The Same to the Same.

COPENHAGEN, Sept. 6, 1795.

GRACIOUS God! it is impossible for me to stifle something like resentment when I receive fresh proofs of your indifference.   What I have suffered this last year is not to be forgotten!   I have not that happy substitute for wisdom, insensibility;

and the lively sympathies which bind me to my fellow-creatures are all of a painful kind. They are the agonies of a broken heart; pleasure and I have shaken hands.

I see here nothing but heaps of ruin, and only converse with people immersed in trade and sensuality.

I am weary of travelling, yet seem to have no home — no resting-place to look to. I am strangely cast off. How often, passing through the rocks, I have thought, "But for this child I would lay my head on one of them and never open my eyes again!" With a heart feelingly alive to all the affections of my nature, I have never met with one softer than the stone that I would fain take for my last pillow. I once thought I had; but it was all a delusion. I meet with families continually, who are bound together by affection or principle; and when I am conscious that I have fulfilled the duties of my station, almost to a forgetfulness of myself, I am ready to demand, in a murmuring tone, of Heaven, "Why am I thus abandoned?"

The Same to the Same.

This letter is written on the night when, driven to madness by Imlay's conduct, Mary Wollstonecraft went out and made the desperate attempt to drown herself in the Thames. The one following this is written soon after her rescue.

LONDON, November, 1795.

I WRITE you now on my knees, imploring you to send my child and the maid with ——, to Paris, to be consigned to the care of Madame ——, Rue ——, Section de ——. Should they be removed, —— can give their direction.

Let the maid have my clothes without distinction.

Pray pay the cook her wages, and do not mention the confession which I forced from her; a little sooner or later is of no consequence. Nothing but my extreme stupidity could have rendered me blind so long. Yet, whilst you assured me that you had no attachment, I thought we might still live together.

I shall make no comments on your conduct, or any appeal to the world. Let my wrongs sleep with me! Soon, very soon, I shall be at peace. When you receive this my burning head will be cold.

I would encounter a thousand deaths rather

than a night like the last. Your treatment has thrown my mind into a state of chaos; yet I am serene. I go to find comfort, and my only fear is, that my poor body will be insulted by an endeavour to recall my hated existence. But I shall plunge into the Thames where there is the least chance of my being snatched from the death I seek.

God bless you! May you never know by experience what you have made me endure. Should your sensibility ever awake, remorse will find its way to your heart; and, in the midst of business and sensual pleasure, I shall appear before you, the victim of your deviation from rectitude.

———◆———

The Same to the Same.

LONDON, November, 1795,
Sunday Morning.

I HAVE only to lament that, when the bitterness of death was past, I was inhumanly brought back to life and misery. But a fixed determination is not to be baffled by disappointment; nor will I allow that to be a frantic attempt which was one of the calmest acts of reason. In this respect I am only accountable to myself. Did I care for what is termed reputation, it is by other circumstances that I should be dishonoured.

You say, " that you know not how to extricate ourselves out of the wretchedness into which we have been plunged." You are extricated long since. But I forbear to comment. If I am condemned to live longer, it is a living death.

It appears to me that you lay much more stress on delicacy than on principle ; for I am unable to discover what sentiment of delicacy would. have been violated by your visiting a wretched friend, if indeed you have any friendship for me. But since your new attachment is the only sacred thing in your eyes, I am silent —. Be happy ! My complaints shall never more damp your enjoyment ; perhaps I am mistaken in supposing that even my death could for more than a moment. This is what you call magnanimity. It is happy for yourself that you possess this quality in the highest degree.

Your continually asserting that you will do all in your power to contribute to my comfort, when you only allude to pecuniary assistance, appears to me a flagrant breach of delicacy. I want not such vulgar comfort, nor will I accept it. I never wanted but your heart. That gone, you have nothing more to give. Had I only poverty to fear, I should not shrink from life. Forgive me then, if I say that I shall consider any direct or indirect attempt to supply my necessities as an insult which I have not merited, and as rather done out of tenderness for your own reputation than for me. Do not mistake me; I do not think that you value money, therefore I will not accept what you do not care for, though I do much less, because certain privations are not painful to me. When I am dead, respect for yourself will make you take care of the child.

I write with difficulty — probably I shall never write to you again. Adieu. God bless you!

———◆———

Shelley to Mary Shelley.

There is very little that is characteristic of the poet SHELLEY to be found in any of his letters which have yet been printed. In a collection of his prose writings edited by his wife, she gives a few letters written to her after they went to reside in Italy. They are printed somewhat fragmentarily, and I have copied them in fragments, leaving out portions which relate to business or uninteresting matters. Shelley does not pour out his heart in his letters, like Keats, nor write to publisher or friends on every trivial occasion, like Byron; and one feels in his letters a reticence of nature which did not unloose itself except in his poetry.

FLORENCE, Thursday, at 11 o'clock,
20 August, 1818.

DEAREST MARY, — We have been delayed in this city four hours for the Austrian minister's passports, but are now on the point of setting out with a vetturino, who engaged to take us on the third day to Padua; that is, we shall only sleep three nights on the road. . . . We have now a comfortable carriage and three mules, and have made very decent bargains to Padua. I should tell you we had delightful fruit for breakfast, — figs very fine, and peaches unfortunately gathered before they were ripe, — whose smell was like what one fancies of the wakening of Paradise flowers.

Well, my dearest Mary, are you very lonely? Tell me the truth, my sweetest, do you ever cry? I shall hear from you in Venice, and once on my return here. If you love me you will keep up your spirits; and, at all events, tell me the truth about them, for I assure you I am not of a disposition to be flattered by your sorrow, though I should be by your cheerfulness, and above all by seeing such fruits of my absence as were produced when we were at Geneva.[1]

What acquaintances have you made? I might have travelled to Padua with a German, who had just come from Rome, and has scarce recovered from a malarial fever caught in the Pontine marshes a week or two since, but I conceded to ——'s entreaties and your absent suggestions and

---

[1] There Mrs. Shelley wrote her famous novel, "Frankenstein."

omitted the opportunity, though I have no great faith in that species of contagion. It is not very hot, not at all too much so for my sensations, and the only thing that inconveniences me is the gnats at night, who roar like so many humming-tops in one's ear.

How is Willmouse and little Clara? They must be kissed for me; and you must particularly remember to speak my name to William, and see that he does not quite forget me, before my return. Adieu, my dearest girl; I think we shall soon meet. I shall write again from Venice. Adieu, dear Mary.

———◆———

The Same to the Same.

Later from Venice he writes her to join him.

I AM going to the bankers to send you money for your journey. Pray come instantly to Este, where I shall be waiting with the utmost anxiety for your arrival. You can pack up directly you get this letter, and employ the next day on that. Then take a vetturino to Florence, to arrive the same evening. From Florence to Este is three days' vetturino journey, and you could not, I think, make it in less by post. I do not think you can, but *try* to get from Florence to Bologna in one day. Do not take the post, for it is not much faster, and very expensive. I have been obliged to decide on all these things without you. I have done for the best; and, my own beloved Mary, you must soon come and scold me if I have done wrong, and kiss me if I have done right; for I am sure I do not know which, and only the event can show. We shall at least be saved the trouble of introduction. I have formed the acquaintance of a lady who is so good, so beautiful, so angelically mild, that were she wise like you, she would be quite a ——. Her eyes are like a reflection of yours. Her manners are like yours when you know and like a person.

Dearest love, be well, be happy, come to me; confide in your own constant and affectionate

P. B. S.

Kiss the blue-eyed darlings for me, and do not let William forget me. Clara cannot recollect me.

———◆———

The Same to the Same.

This little note, written a year before his death, when Mary sent him her picture, is among Shelley's latest letters to his wife.

RAVENNA, Aug. 15, 1821.

MY DEAREST LOVE, — I accept your present of your picture, and wish you would get it prettily framed for me. I will wear for your sake upon my heart this image which is ever present to my mind.

I have only two minutes to write; the post is just setting off. I shall leave this place Thursday or Friday. You would forgive my longer stay if you knew the fight I have had to make it so short. I need not say where my own feeling impels me.

It still remains fixed that Lord Byron should come to Tuscany, — if possible, Pisa.

Your faithful and affectionate   S.

—◆—

Byron to the Countess Guicciola.

It was in the autumn of 1818 that Lord Byron met with Teresa Guicciola. She was a little more than eighteen years old, — a golden-haired Italian woman, such as Titian loved to paint, — and had recently been taken from the convent in which she was reared, to be married to Count Guicciola, a wealthy widower of sixty. Moore says, in his *Life of Byron:* "The love that sprung up between Byron and Madame Guicciola was instantaneous and mutual, though with the usual disproportion of sacrifice between the two. . . . The fount of natural tenderness in his soul, which neither the world's efforts nor his own had been able to chill or choke up, was, with something of its first freshness, set flowing once more. He knew what it was to love and to be loved, — too late, it is true, for happiness and too wrongly for peace, but with devotion enough on the part of the woman to satisfy even his thirst for affection, and on his own part with a sad earnestness, a foreboding fidelity, which made him cling the more passionately to this attachment from feeling it would be his last."

In one of the Countess Guicciola's absences from home, he was fond of sitting alone in her garden; and, finding there one day a copy of *Corinne*, which she had been reading, he wrote, in English, this letter on one of the fly-leaves of the book.

Bologna, Aug. 25, 1819.

My dearest Teresa, — I have read this book in your garden. My love, you were absent, or else I could not have read it. It is a favourite book of yours, and the writer was a friend of mine. You will not understand these English words, and others will not understand them, which is the reason I have not scrawled them in Italian; but you will recognize the handwriting of him who passionately loved you, and you will divine that over a book which was yours he could only think of love. In that word, beautiful in all languages, but most so in yours, — *Amor mio,* — is comprised my existence here and hereafter. I feel I exist here, and I fear that I shall exist hereafter — to what purpose you will decide; my destiny rests with you, and you are a woman, eighteen years of age, and two out of a convent.

I wish that you had stayed there, with all my heart, — or, at least, that I had never met you in your married state.

But all this is too late. I love you and you love me, — at least, you say so and act as if you did so, which last is a great consolation in all events. But I more than love you, and cannot cease to love you.

Think of me sometimes when the Alps and the ocean divide us; but they never will, unless you wish it.

BYRON.

———◆———

Charlotte Carpenter to Walter Scott.

Walter Scott had had a disappointment in a love affair in which his feelings seem to have been deeply engaged, when his heart was caught in the rebound by Miss CHARLOTTE CARPENTER, a lively brunette, of French birth and parentage, the ward of an English marquis, Lord Downshire, who, in the spring of 1797, was travelling in Scotland. Scott and Miss Carpenter were engaged in the fall of this year, and these letters are written by Miss Carpenter to her betrothed just before marriage. There was only a little delay after the engagement, to get Lord Downshire's consent, and to settle the minds of Scott's family on the subject of the lady's fortune and birth.

Mrs. Scott, without any great surplus of romance or sentiment, as would appear from her letters, was a lively and cheerful-tempered wife. She never seems to have had

any very deep appreciation of her husband's genius, and
when his fame as the great novelist was widening, she is
said to have regarded his genius largely as a means for
refurnishing the drawing-room or adding a new wing to the
house. She was, however, a faithful and capable helpmeet, even if she lacked those finer sympathies which are
so rare, even in the happiest lives. The following notes
were written just before the marriage, and have a good
deal of girlish vivacity, which was, no doubt, very capti-
vating to the young Scottish lawyer.

CARLISLE, Oct. 25, 1797.

INDEED, Mr. Scott, I am by no means pleased
with all this writing. I have told you how much
I dislike it, and yet you still persist in asking me
to write, and that by return of post. Oh, you
really are quite out of your senses! I should not
have indulged you in that whim of yours, had you
not given me the hint that my silence gives an
air of mystery. I have no reason that can detain
me from acquainting you that my father and
mother were French, of the name of Charpentier.
He had a place under government; their residence
was at Lyons, where you would find on inquiries
that they lived in good repute, and *in very good
style.* I had the misfortune of losing my father
before I could know the value of such a parent.
At his death we were left to the care of Lord
Downshire, who was his very great friend, and

very soon I had the affliction of losing my mother. Our taking the name of Carpenter was on my brother's going to India, to prevent any little difficulties that might have occurred. I hope now you are pleased. Lord D. could have given every information, as he has been acquainted with all my family. You say you almost love *him*, but until your *almost* becomes to a *quite*, I cannot love *you*. Before I conclude this famous epistle, I will give you a little hint, — that is, not to put so many *musts* in your letters. It is beginning *rather too* soon; and another thing is that I take the liberty not to mind them much, but I expect you to mind me. You *must* take care of yourself. You *must* think of me, and believe me

Yours sincerely

C. C.

The Same to the Same.

CARLISLE, Nov. 14, 1797.

YOUR letter never could have come in a more favourable moment. Anything you could have said would have been well received. You surprise me much at the regret you express you had before leaving Carlisle. Indeed, I can't believe it was on my account. I was so uncommonly stupid I don't know what could be the matter with me; I was so very low, and felt really ill. It was even a trouble to speak. The settling of our little plans, all looked so much in earnest, that I began reflecting more seriously than I generally do, *or approve of.* I don't think that very thoughtful people can ever be happy. As this is my maxim, adieu to all thoughts. I have made a determination to be pleased with everything and with everybody in Edinburgh,— a wise system for happiness, is it not? I enclose the lock. I have had almost all my hair cut off. Miss Nicholson has taken some, which she has sent to London to be made into something, but this you are not to know of, as she intends it as a present for you. I am happy to hear of your father's being better pleased as to money matters; it will come at last, don't let that trifle disturb you. Adieu, Monsieur. J'ai l'honneur d'être votre très humble et très

Obéissante

C. C.

———◆———

The Same to the Same.

CARLISLE, Nov. 27, 1797.

You have made me very *triste* all day. Pray, never more complain of being poor. Are you not ten times richer than I? Depend upon yourself and your profession. I have no doubt you will rise very high, and be a *great rich man*, but we should look down to be contented with our lot and banish all disagreeable thoughts. We shall do very well. I am sorry to hear you have such a *bad head;* I hope I shall nurse away all your aches. I think you write too much ; when I am mistress I shall not allow it. How very angry I should be with you if you were to part with *Leonore!* [1] Do you really believe I should think it an *unnecessary expense* where your health and pleasure could be concerned? I have a better opinion of you, and I am very glad you don't give up the cavalry, as I *love anything that is stylish.*

Don't forget to find a stand for the old carriage, as I shall like to keep it in case we go on any journey ; it is so much more convenient than the postchaises, and will do very well till we can keep our carriage. What an idea of yours that was to mention where you wish to have your *bones laid !* If you were married I should think you were tired of me. A very pretty compliment *before marriage !* I hope sincerely I shall not live to see that day. If you always have such cheerful thoughts, how

[1] Scott's horse, named for Burger's ballad, which he had just translated.

very pleasant and gay you must be! Adieu, my dearest friend; take care of yourself if you love me, as I have no wish that you should *visit* that *beautiful* and *romantic* scene, the burying-place. Adieu, once more, and believe that you are loved very sincerely by

C. C.

——◆——

The Same to the Same.

CARLISLE, Dec. 10, 1797.

IF I could but really believe that my letter only gave you half the pleasure you express, I almost think, my dearest Scott, that I should get very fond of writing, just to indulge you, — that is saying a great deal. I hope you are sensible of the compliment I pay you, and don't expect I shall always be so pretty behaved. You may depend on me, my dearest friend, for fixing as *early* a day as I possibly can, and if it happens not to be so soon as you could wish, you must not be angry with me. It is very unlucky you are such a bad housekeeper, as I am no better. I shall try. I hope very soon to have the pleasure of seeing you, and of telling you how much I love you; but I wish the first fortnight was over. With all my love, and all sorts of pretty things, adieu.

CHARLOTTE.

P. S. Étudiez votre Français. Remember you are to teach me Italian in return, but I shall be a stupid scholar.

———◆——

The Same to the Same.

CARLISLE, Dec. 14, 1797.
(A week before marriage.)

. . . I HEARD last night from my friends in London, and I shall certainly have the deed this week. I will send it to you directly ; but not to lose so much time as you have been reckoning, I will postpone any little delay that might happen by the post by fixing next Wednesday for your coming here, and on Thursday, the 21st, O my dear Scott, — on that day I shall be yours forever.

C. C.

P. S. Arrange so that we shall see none of your family the night of our arrival. I shall be so tired and such a fright, I shall not be seen to advantage.

———◆——

Leigh Hunt to his Betrothed.

This letter was written by LEIGH HUNT to his betrothed three or four years before their marriage, when he was just beginning to be known in literary and journalistic circles. He was not more than twenty-two when he was engaged to be married, and his Marienne at this date could not have been more than sixteen, so that the faults of handwriting and blotting-about which he lectures her, may be pardoned in one who was still a school-girl.

GAINSBOROUGH, Thursday,
February, 1806.

DEAREST GIRL, — My journey to Doncaster is deferred till next week, so I sit down to write you a day earlier than I intended, in order that you may have two letters instead of one this week to make up for former deficiencies. A very heavy rain last night has made the snow vanish from the fields, which look delightfully green this morning. I walked out to enjoy the lively air and the universal sunshine, and seated myself with a book on the gateway at the bottom of a little eminence covered with evergreens, a little way from Gainsborough. It seemed the return of spring; a flock of sheep were grazing before me, and cast up every now and then their inquiring visages as much as to say, "What singular being is that so intent upon the mysterious thin substance he is turning over with his hand?" The crows at intervals came wheeling with long cawings above my head; the herds lowed from the surrounding farms; the windmills whirled to the breeze, flinging their huge and rapid shadows on the fields; and the river Trent sparkled in the sun from east

to .west. A delightful serenity diffused itself·
through my heart. I worshipped the magnificence
and the love of the God of nature, and I thought
of *you*. These two sensations always arise in my
heart in the quiet of a rural landscape, and I have
often considered it a proof of the purity and the
reality of my affection for you, that it always feels
most powerful in my religious moments. And this
is very natural. Are you not the greatest blessing
Heaven has bestowed upon me? Your image at-
tends my rural rambles not only in the healthful
walks when, escaped from the clamour of streets
and the glare of theatres, I am ready to exclaim
with Cowper, " God made the country, and man
made the town." It is present with me even in
the bustle of life ; it gives me a distaste to a frivolous and riotous society ; it excites me to improve myself in order to deserve your affection,
and it quenches the little flashes of caprice and
impatience which disturb the repose of existence.
If I feel my anger rising at trifles it checks me in-
stantaneously ; it seems to say to me, " Why do
you disturb yourself ? Marienne loves you ; you
deserve her love, and ought to be above these
little marks of a little mind." Such is the power
of love. I am naturally a man of violent passions,
but your affection has taught me to subdue them.

Whenever you feel any little inquietudes or impatiences arising in your bosom, think of the happiness you bestow upon me, and real love will produce the same effect on you that it produces on me. *No reasoning person ought to marry, who cannot say, " My love has made me better, and more desirous of improvement than I was before."*

. . . I do not write, I acknowledge, with the best hand in the world, but I endeavour to avoid blots or interpolations. I suppose you guess by this preamble that I am going to find fault with your letters. I would not dare, however, to find fault were I not sure that you would receive my letters cheerfully. You have no false shame to induce you to conceal or deny your faults, — quite the contrary ; you think sometimes too much of them, for I know of none which you cannot remedy. Besides, my faithful and attentive affection would induce me to ask with confidence any little sacrifice of your time and care ; and as you have done so much for me in correcting the errors of my *head* you will not feel very unpleasant when I venture to correct the errors of your hand. Now, cannot you sit down on Sunday, my sweet girl, and write me a fair, even-minded, honest *hand*, unvexed with desperate blots or skulking interlineations? Mind, I do not quarrel with the contents or with the subject; what you tell me of others amuses me, and what you tell me of yourself delights me. It is merely the fashion of your lines; in short, as St. Paul saith, "It is the *spirit* giveth life, but the *letter* killeth."

Present my respects to Mrs. Hunter and tell her I have found the tune, the Scotch tune, which pleased her so much between the acts in *Douglas;* it belongs to a song called Tweedside, beginning, "What beauties does Flora disclose." I will play it to her when I return. I shall write Mrs. Hunter next week. . . . It is astonishing I should ever be melancholy when I possess friends like these; and when, above all, I am able to tell my dearest Marienne how infinitely she is beloved by her

HENRY.

———◆———

Keats's Letters to Fanny Brawne.

Among the saddest of sad letters are those of JOHN KEATS to Fanny Brawne. These letters, written under the shadow that impended over the last two years of his life, are touched by the double sadness of love and of death.

He met Fanny Brawne in the fall of 1818, and a little later he wrote to a friend: "I never was in love, and yet the shape of a woman has haunted me these two days. . . . This morning poetry has conquered. I have relapsed into those abstractions that are my only life. I feel escaped

from a new, strange, threatening sorrow, and I am thankful
for it. There is an awful warmth about my heart like a
load of immortality." It is difficult to infer, from what we
can find out about Fanny Brawne, whether she was even
in beauty the creature that the poet fancied, or whether his
ideal was not created bodily out of his own poet's imagin-
ings. That she was shallow-hearted, with sympathies and
brain as shallow as her heart, a person with any of the in-
tuitions of sentiment cannot fail to infer from everything
that is to be learned of her. What can be said of a woman who, ten years after Keats's death, could write of him
to a friend that "the kindest act would be to let him rest
forever in the obscurity to which circumstances have condemned him"? — a woman who had neither love enough
nor sense enough to guess at the greatness that had stooped
so to idealize her; who could speak thus flippantly of a
poet whom Matthew Arnold and other critics name to-day
in the same breath with Shakespeare, for the debt which
is owed him by English poetry.

Keats could not escape the shape that haunted him,
whether he would or no. In February, 1819, they were
engaged, and for a year he either lived near her so as to
see her almost daily, or he wrote her every day such letters
as these that follow, — letters in which his passion for her
is blended with his passionate sense of beauty and his
passionate longing for death. "I have two luxuries to
brood over," he writes her, — "your loveliness and the hour
of my death."

In the winter of 1820 death came near enough for the
poet to feel his presence. One night after a slight cough-
ing-fit, feeling his mouth fill with blood, he said, "Bring
me the candle," then looked at the blood calmly with an

eye that had been trained by his medical studies to know the symptoms of disease.

"I know the colour of that blood," he said ; " it is arterial I cannot be deceived in that colour; that drop is my death-warrant, — I must die." Yet at that moment, above all things, he thought of *her*. " When I felt it possible I might not survive, at that moment I thought of nothing but you. When I said, ' This is unfortunate,' I thought of you." In his lonely and wakeful nights later in his illness, thoughts of her haunted him, mingled with other thoughts, — that he had done no immortal work such as he had hoped to do, that he had not made a name to be remembered; only, he adds consolingly to himself, "I have truly loved the spirit of beauty in all things."

In the autumn of 1820 it was decided he should go to Italy, and his faithful friend Severn went with him and remained with him till he died. The letters to Fanny Brawne end with the two which are quoted last in this series, — the two he wrote before he went to Italy after their parting ; but his letters to his friends are filled with that anguish and longing of the heart that tears him when-ever he thinks of her. "I can bear to die ; I *cannot* bear to leave her," he cries. " The very thing I want to live for will be a great occasion of my death. . . . I wish for death every day and night to deliver me from these pains, and then I wish death away, for death would destroy these pains, which are better than nothing." Again, " Oh that I could be buried near where *she* lives ! I am afraid to write to her, to receive a letter from her ; *to see her handwriting would break my heart. Even to hear of her, to see her name written, would be more than I can bear.* Where can I look for conso-lation or ease ? If I had any chance of recovery, this

passion would kill me." Not very long after these words.
were written, the tortured, restless heart was still, and in a
few months the daisies, whose tender roots he had felt
piercing his grave before he lay asleep there, were cover-
ing him over with their quietness and peace.

Keats to Fanny Brawne.

NEWPORT, 10th July, 1819.

MY SWEET GIRL, — Your letter gave me more
delight than anything in the world but yourself
could do; indeed, I am almost astonished that
any absent one should have that luxurious power
over my senses which I feel. Even when I am
not thinking of you I receive your influence and
a tenderer nature stealing upon me. All my
thoughts, my unhappiest days and nights, have,
I find, not at all cured me of my love of Beauty,
but made it so intense that I am miserable that
you are not with me; or, rather, breathe in that
dull sort of patience that cannot be called Life.
I never knew before what such a love as you have
made me feel was. I did not believe in it; my
fancy was afraid of it, lest it should burn me up.
But if you will fully love me, though there may be
some fire, 't will not be more than we can bear,
when moistened and bedewed with Pleasures.
You mention "horrid people," and ask me
whether it depend upon them whether I see you

again. Do understand me, my love, in this. I
have so much of you in my heart that I must turn
Mentor when I see a chance of harm befalling
you. I would never see anything but Pleasure in
your eyes, love on your lips, and Happiness in
your steps. I would wish to see you among
those amusements suitable to your inclinations
and spirits; so that our loves might be a delight
in the midst of Pleasures agreeable enough, rather
than a resource from vexations and cares. But I
doubt much, in case of the worst, whether I shall
be philosopher enough to follow my own Lessons;
if I saw my resolution give you pain, I could not.
Why may I not speak of your Beauty, since without that I could never have loved you? I cannot conceive any beginning of such love as I have
for you but Beauty. There may be a sort of love
for which, without the least sneer at it, I have
the highest respect, and can admire it in others;
but it has not the richness, the bloom, the full
form, the enchantment, of love after my own
heart. So let me speak of your Beauty, though
to my own endangering, if you could be so cruel
as to try elsewhere its Power. You say you are
afraid I shall think you do not love me; in saying
this you make me ache the more to be near you.
I am at the diligent use of my faculties here, —

I do not pass a day without sprawling some blank verse or tagging some rhymes; and here I must confess that (since I am on that subject) I love you the more in that I believe that you have liked me for my own sake and for nothing else. I have met with women who I really think would like to be married to a Poem and to be given away by a Novel.

I have seen your Comet, and only wish it was a sign that poor Rice would get well, whose illness makes him rather a melancholy companion; and the more so as so to conquer his feelings and hide them from me with a forced Pun. I kissed your writing over in the hope you had indulged me by leaving a trace of honey. What was your dream? Tell it me and I will tell you the interpretation thereof.

Ever yours, my love,

JOHN KEATS.

———◆———

The Same to the Same.

25 COLLEGE STREET, 13 Oct., 1819.

MY DEAREST GIRL, — This moment I have set myself to copy some verses out fair. I cannot proceed with any degree of content. I must write you a line or two, and see if that will assist in

dismissing you from my Mind for ever so short a
time. Upon my Soul, I can think of nothing else.
The time is past when I had power to advise and
warn you against the unpromising morning of my
Life. My love has made me selfish. I cannot
exist without you. I am forgetful of everything
but seeing you again; my Life seems to stop
there; I see no further. You have absorbed me.
I have a sensation at the present moment as though
I was dissolving. I should be exquisitely miserable without the hope of soon seeing you. I should
be afraid to separate myself far from you. My
sweet Fanny, will your heart never change? My
love, will it? I have no limit now to my love.
... Your note came in just here. I cannot be
happier away from you. — 'T is richer than an
argosy of pearls. Do not threat me, even in jest.
I have been astonished that men could die Mar-
tyrs for religion, — I have shuddered at it. I
shudder no more; I could be-martyred for my
Religion, — love is my religion, — I could die for
that. I could die for you. My Creed is Love,
and you are its only tenet. . You have ravished
me away by a Power I cannot resist; and yet I
could resist till I saw you; and even since I have
seen you I have endeavoured often " to reason
against the reasons of my Love." I can do that

11

no more, — the pain would be too great. My love is selfish. I cannot breathe without you.

Yours forever,

JOHN KEATS.

———◆———

The Same to the Same.

FEBRUARY, 1820 (?).

MY DEAREST GIRL, — If illness makes such an agreeable variety in the manner of your eyes, I should wish you sometimes to be ill. I wish I had read your note before you went last night, that I might have assured you how far I was from suspecting any coldness. You had a just right to be a little silent to one who speaks so plainly to you. You must believe — you shall, you will — that I can do nothing, say nothing, think nothing of you but what has its spring in the Love which has so long been my pleasure and torment. On the night I was taken ill — when so violent a rush of blood came to my Lungs that I felt nearly suffocated — I assure you I felt it possible I might not survive, and at that moment thought of nothing but you. When I said to Brown, "This is unfortunate," I thought of you. 'T is true that since the first two or three days other subjects have entered my head. I shall be looking forward to Health and the Spring and a regular routine of our old Walks.

Your affectionate   J. K.

The Same to the Same.

1820.

MY DEAR FANNY, — Do not let your mother suppose that you hurt me by writing at night. For some reason or other your last night's note was not so treasurable as former ones. I would fain that you call me *Love* still. To see you happy and in high spirits is a great consolation to me; still let me believe that you are not half so happy as my restoration would make you. I am nervous, I own, and may think myself worse than I really am; if so, you must indulge me, and pamper with that sort of tenderness you have manifested towards me in different Letters. My sweet creature, when I look back upon the pains and torments I have suffered for you from the day I left you to go to the Isle of Wight, the ecstasies in which I have passed some days and the miseries in their turn, I wonder the more at the Beauty which has kept up the spell so fervently. When I send this round I shall be in the front parlour watching to see you show yourself for a minute in the garden. How illness stands as a barrier betwixt me and you! Even if I was well — I must make myself as good a Philosopher as possible. Now I have had opportunities of passing nights anxious and awake, I have found other thoughts intrude upon me. "If I should die," said I to myself, "I have left no immortal work behind me, — nothing to make my friends proud of my memory, — but I have loved the principle of beauty in all things, and if I had had time I would have made myself remembered." Thoughts like these came. very feebly whilst I was in health, and every pulse beat for you; now you divide with this (may *I* say it?) "last infirmity of noble minds" all my reflection.

God bless you, love!

J. KEATS.

———◆———

The Same to the Same.

1820.

SWEETEST FANNY, — You fear sometimes I do not love you so much as you wish? My dear girl, I love you ever and ever and without reserve. The more I have known the more have I loved. In every way, — even my jealousies have been agonies of Love; in the hottest fit I ever had I would have died for you. I have vexed you too much. But for Love! Can I help it? You are always new. The last of your kisses was ever the sweetest, the last smile the brightest, the last movement the gracefulest. When you passed my window, home yesterday, I was filled with as much admiration as if I had seen you for the first time. You uttered a half complaint once that I only loved your beauty. Have I nothing else, then, to love in you but that? Do not I see a heart naturally furnished with wings imprison itself with me? No ill prospect has been able to turn your thoughts a moment from me. This perhaps should be as much a subject of sorrow as joy, — but I will not talk of that. Even if you did not love me I could not help an entire devotion to you; how much more deeply, then, must I feel for you, knowing you love me. My Mind has been the most discontented and restless one that ever was put into a body too small for it. I never felt my Mind repose upon anything with complete and undistracted enjoyment — upon no person but you. When you are in the room my thoughts never fly out of window; you always concentrate my whole senses. The anxiety shown about our Loves in your last note is an immense pleasure to me; however you must not suffer such speculations to molest you any more; nor will I any more believe you can have the least pique against me. Brown is gone out, but here is Mrs. Wylie; when she is gone I shall be awake for you. Remembrances to your Mother.

Your affectionate

J. KEATS.

The Same to the Same.

MY DEAREST FANNY, — I slept well last night,
and am no worse this morning for it. Day by day,
if I am not deceived, I get a more unrestrained use
of my Chest. The nearer a racer gets to the Goal
the more his anxiety becomes; so I, lingering
upon the borders of health, feel my impatience
increase. Perhaps on your account I have imagined my illness more serious than it is : how horrid
was the chance of slipping into the ground instead
of into your arms — the difference is amazing,
Love. Death must come at last; Man must die
as Shallow says; but before that is my fate I fain
would try what more pleasures than you have
given, so sweet a creature as you can give. Let
me have another opportunity of years before me
and I will not die without being remembered.
Take care of yourself, dear, that we may both be
well in the Summer. I do not at all fatigue myself with writing, having merely put a line or two
here and there, — a Task which would worry a
stout state of the body and mind, but which just
suits me, as I can do no more.

Your affectionate

J. K.

The Same to the Same.

SEPTEMBER (?), 1820.

MY DEAREST FANNY, — My head is puzzled this morning, and I scarce know what I shall say, though I am full of a hundred things. 'T is certain I would rather be writing to you this morning, notwithstanding the alloy of grief in such an occupation, than enjoy any other pleasure, with health to boot, unconnected with you. Upon my soul I have loved you to the extreme. I wish you could know the tenderness with which I continually brood over your different aspects of countenance, action, and dress. I see you come down in the morning; I see you meet me at the window, — I see everything over again eternally that I ever have seen. If I get on the pleasant clue, I live in a sort of happy misery; if on the unpleasant, 't is misery. You complain of my ill-treating you in word, thought, and deed. I am sorry; at times I feel bitterly sorry that I ever made you unhappy. My excuse is that those words have been wrung from me by the sharpness of my feelings. At all events and in any case I have been wrong; could I believe that I did it without any cause, I should be the most sincere of Penitents. I could give way to my repentant feelings now, I could recant all my suspicions, I could mingle with you heart and Soul, though absent, were it not for some parts of your Letters. Do you suppose it possible I could ever leave you? You know what I think of myself and what of you. You know that I should feel how much it was my loss and how little yours. My friends laugh at you? I know some of them; when I know them all, I shall never think of them again as friends or even acquaintances. My friends have behaved well to me in every instance but one, and there they have become tattlers and inquisitors into my conduct; spying upon a secret I would rather die than share it with anybody's confidence. For this I cannot wish them well, I care not to see any of them again. If I am the theme, I will not be the Friend of idle Gossips. Good gods, what a shame it is our Loves should be so put into the microscope of a Coterie! Their laughs should not affect you (I may perhaps give you reasons some day for these laughs, for I suspect a few people to hate me well enough, *for reasons I know of*, who have pretended a great friendship for me) when in competition with one who if he should never see you again would make you the saint of his memory. These Laughers, who do not like you, who envy you for your beauty, who would have God-blessed me from you forever; who were plying me with disencouragements with respect to you eternally. People are revengeful; do not mind them; do nothing but love me. If I knew that for certain, life and health will in such event be a heaven, and death itself will be less painful. I long to believe in immortality. I shall never be able to bid you an entire farewell. If I am destined to be happy with you here, how short is the longest Life! I wish to believe in immortality, I wish to live with you forever. Do not let my name ever pass between you and these laughers; if I have no other merit than the great Love for you, that were sufficient to keep me sacred and unmentioned in such society. If I have been cruel and unjust, I swear my love has ever been greater than my cruelty, which lasts but a minute, whereas my Love, come what will, shall last forever. If concession to me has hurt your Pride, God knows I have had little pride in my heart when thinking of you. Your name never passes my lips; do not let mine pass yours. Those People do not like me. After reading my Letter you even then wish to see me. I am strong enough to walk over, but I dare not. I shall feel so much pain in parting with you again. My dearest love, I am afraid to see you; I am strong, but not strong enough to see you. Will my arm be ever round you again, and if so shall I be obliged to leave you again? My

sweet Love! I am happy whilst I believe your
first Letter. Let me be but certain that you are
mine heart and soul, and I could die more happily than I could otherwise live. If you think
me cruel, if you think I have slighted you, do
muse it over again and see into my heart. My
love to you is "true as truth's simplicity and
simpler than the infancy of truth," as I think I
once said before. How could I slight you? How
threaten to leave you? not in the spirit of a Threat
to you, — no; but in the spirit of Wretchedness
in myself. My fairest, my delicious, my angel
Fanny! do not believe me such a vulgar fellow.
I will be as patient in illness and as believing in
love as I am able.

Yours forever, my dearest,

JOHN KEATS.

———◆———

The Last Letter of Keats written before his Departure.

SEPTEMBER (?), 1820.

I do not write this till the last, that no eye may
catch it.[1]

MY DEAREST GIRL, — I wish you could invent
some means to make me happy without you.
Every hour I am more and more concentrated in
you; everything else tastes like chaff in my

[1] He had added the words "My dearest Girl," after
writing the letter.

mouth. I feel it almost impossible to go to Italy: the fact is I cannot leave you, and shall never taste one minute's content until it pleases chance to let me live with you for good. But I will not go on at this rate. A person in health as you are can have no conception of the horrors that nerves and a temper like mine go through. What Island do your friends propose retiring to? I should be happy to go there with you alone, but in company I should object to it; the backbitings and jealousies of new colonists who have nothing else to amuse themselves, is unbearable. Mr. Dilke came to see me yesterday, and gave me a great deal more pain than pleasure. I shall never be able any more to endure the society of any of those who used to meet at Elm Cottage and Wentworth Place. The last two years taste like brass upon my Palate. If I cannot live with you I will live alone. I do not think my health will improve much while I am separated from you. For all this I am averse to seeing you, — I cannot bear flashes of light and return into my gloom again. I am not so unhappy now as I should be if I had seen you yesterday. To be happy with you seems such an impossibility! it requires a luckier star than mine; it will never be. I enclose a passage from one of your letters which I want you to alter a little. I want (if you will have it so) the matter

expressed less coldly to me. If my health would
bear it, I could write a poem which I have in my
head, which would be a consolation for people in
such a situation as mine. I would show some one
in Love as I am, with a person living in such Liberty as you do. Shakespeare always sums up matters in the most sovereign manner. Hamlet's heart
was full of such misery as mine is when he said
to Ophelia, " Go to a nunnery, go, go ! " Indeed
I should like to give up the matter at once, — I
should like to die. I am sickened at the brute
world which you are smiling with. I hate men,
and women more. I see nothing but thorns for
the future; wherever I may be next winter, in
Italy or nowhere, Brown will be living near you
with his indecencies. I see no prospect of any
rest. Suppose me in Rome — well, I should there
see you as in a magic glass going to and from
town at all hours. I wish you could infuse a little
confidence of human nature into my heart. I cannot muster any; the world is too brutal for me.
I am glad there is such a thing as the grave ; I am
sure I shall never have any rest till I get there.
At any rate I will indulge myself by never seeing
any more Dilke or Brown, or any of their Friends.
I wish I was either in your arms full of faith or
that a Thunderbolt would strike me.

God bless you ! J. K.

William Hazlitt to Sarah L.

WILLIAM HAZLITT, the poet-essayist, and one of the finest critics of his time, was a man of keen sensibility, with the poetic tendency to idealize some of the commonest things of earth into visions of beauty and objects of rapturous adoration. In one of these moods he met with a young woman, the daughter of his lodging-house keeper, for whom he entertained an affection as mad as it was hopeless. He would have married her if she would have consented to become his wife, but she seems not to have been sensible of the honour he would have done her, and to have merely played with his feelings as the amusement of her unoccupied mornings, in which she would sometimes remain beside him while he ate the breakfast which she served him with her fair hands. Hazlitt paints her as a vision of rarest beauty, somewhat undeveloped and soulless, but into whom, like Pygmalion, his devotion would infuse life and soul. The truth seems to be, that his statue was a vulgar young woman, accustomed to flirt with the lodgers who came under her mother's roof, and that she could no more understand the feeling with which she was regarded by a man of genius than she could have returned it if it had been comprehensible to her. The following, like some of Keats's letters, opens so deep the heart of the writer that it would seem too personal to print it, if Hazlitt had not himself published an account of this unhappy episode in his life, and included in it the few letters which he wrote to Sarah L.

MARCH, 1822.

You will be glad to learn that I have done my work, — a volume in less than a month. That is

one reason why I am better than when I came ;
and another is, I have had two letters from Sarah.

I walk out of an afternoon and hear the birds
sing, as I told you, and think if I had you hanging
on my arm, and that for life, how happy I should
be, happier than I ever hoped to be, or had any
conception of till I knew you. " But that can
never be," I hear you answer in a soft, low murmur. Well, let me dream of it sometimes. I
am not happy too often, except when that favourite note, the harbinger of spring, recalling the
hopes of my youth, whispers thy name and peace
together in my ear. I was reading something
about Mr. Macready to-day, and this puts me in
mind of that delicious night when I went with
your mother and you to see " Romeo and Juliet."
Can I forget it for a moment? — your sweet, modest looks, your infinite propriety of behaviour, all
your sweet, winning ways, your hesitating about
taking my arm, as we came out, till your mother
did, your laughing about nearly losing your cloak,
your stepping into the coach, and oh, my sitting
down beside you there, — *you*, whom I had loved
so long, so well, — and your assuring me I had
not lessened your pleasure at the play by being
with you, and giving me your dear hand to press
in mine !

I thought I was in heaven! That slender form contained my all of heaven upon earth; and as I folded you — yes, you, my own Sarah — to my bosom, there was, as you say, a tie between us. You did seem to me, for those few short moments, to be mine in all truth, honour, and sacredness. Oh that we could be always so! Do not mock me, for I am a very child in love. I ought to beg pardon for behaving so ill afterwards, but I hope the little image made it all up between us.

This letter is endorsed: —

"To this letter I received no answer, not a line. The rolling years of eternity will never fill up that blank."

That Hazlitt suffered greatly from this melancholy passion is not to be doubted. He writes to one of his friends whom he makes his confidant: "The sky is marble to my thoughts; nature is dead around me, as hope is within me. No object can give me one gleam of satisfaction now, nor the prospect of it in time to come. I wander by the seaside, and the eternal ocean, and lasting despair, and *her* face are ever before me. Slighted by her on whom my heart by its last fibre hung, where shall I turn? I wake with her by my side, not as my sweet bedfellow, but as the corpse of my love, without a heart in her bosom, cold, insensible, or struggling away from me; and the worm gnaws me, and the sting of unrequited love, and the canker of a hopeless, endless sorrow. I have lost the taste of food by my feverish anxiety; and my favourite beverage, which used to refresh me when I rose, has no moisture in it. Oh, cold, solitary, sepulchral breakfasts, compared to those which I had promised myself with her; or which I made when she had been standing an hour by my side, my guardian angel, my wife, my sweet friend, my Eve, my all! and had blessed me with her seraph kisses."

PART II.

LETTERS OF ROYAL PERSONAGES.

What were life without affection? Without Love, I can fancy no gentleman. — THACKERAY.

PART II.

LETTERS OF ROYAL PERSONAGES.

Letters of Henry VIII. to Anne Boleyn.

AMONG all the collections of old love-letters there is none which has elicited more interest and curiosity than that of HENRY VIII. to his second queen, ANNE BOLEYN. These letters are supposed to have been stolen from her during her brief queenship, and were found, years after, in the library of the Vatican in Rome. Most of them were written in French, although one or two are in English. They are as ardent as anything in the history of courtship, and show the king as passionate in following his inclinations as he was earnest in annulling any ties he had formed, after his ardour had cooled.

These letters were written while Anne was retired from court, under her father's protection, in the same year in which the king's marriage with her was celebrated.

1528.

MY MISTRESS AND FRIEND, — My heart and I surrender ourselves into your hands, beseeching you to hold us commended to your favour, and that by absence your affection to us may not be

lessened; for it would be a great pity to increase
our pain, of which absence produces enough and
more than I could ever have thought could be
felt; reminding us of a point of astronomy, which
is this,—the longer the days are the more distant
is the sun, and nevertheless the hotter; so it is
with our love, for by absence we are kept at a
distance from one another, and yet it retains its
fervour at least on my side. I hope the like on
yours, assuring you that on my part the pain of
absence is already too great for me; and when I
think of the increase of that which I am forced to
suffer, it would be almost intolerable, but for the
firm hope I have of your unchangeable affection
for me. And to remind you of this sometimes, and
seeing that I cannot be personally present with
you, I now send you the nearest thing I can to
that, namely, my picture set in bracelets with the
whole of the device, which you already know, wishing I were in their place when it should please you.

This is from the hand of your loyal servant and
friend,

H., R.

—◆—

The Same to the Same.

1528.

THE approach of the time for which I have so
long waited rejoices me so much, that it seems

almost to have come already. However, the entire accomplishment cannot be till the two persons meet, which meeting is more desired by me than anything in this world; for what joy can be greater upon earth than to have the company of her who is dearest to me, knowing likewise that she does the same on her part, the thought of which gives me the greatest pleasure.

Judge what an effect the presence of that person must have on me, whose absence has grieved my heart more than either words or writing can express and which nothing can cure, but that begging you, my mistress, to tell your father from me, that I desire him to hasten the day appointed by two days, that he may be at court before the old term, or at farthest on the day prefixed, for otherwise I shall think he will not do the lover's turn, as he said he would, nor answer my expectation.

No more at present for lack of time, hoping shortly that by word of mouth I shall tell you the rest of the sufferings endured by me from your absence.

Written by the hand of the secretary, who wishes himself at this moment privately with you, and who is, and always will be,

Your loyal and most assured servant,

H. no other (A. B.) seeks, R.

Anne Boleyn to Henry VIII.

I have not been able to find any English copy from the original of the following letter. It is translated from a Life of Queen Elizabeth, in Italian, by Gregorio Leti, who claims that it is from authentic sources. Miss Strickland, in her Life of Anne Boleyn, and some other historians, have doubted its genuineness. Miss Strickland refuses to accept it on the ground that it is "too fulsome" a letter for Anne Boleyn's lofty pride of character to dictate. But this is not good ground for disproving such a letter in the age of Henry VIII. or Queen Elizabeth, when such fulsome flattery of the sovereign was so common even from noble minds. This letter sounds rather like the natural adulation of a young and ambitious girl who had been flattered by the boldly expressed admiration of a great king. Leti dates it in 1519, but this would certainly be much too early, as she did not return from France, where she had passed part of her girlhood, till long after that time.

It is supposed that King Henry met her at her father's house not long after her return, and that it was through his influence she was made maid of honour to Queen Katherine.

No date.

SIR, — It belongs only to the august mind of a great king, to whom Nature has given a heart full of generosity towards the sex, to repay by favours so extraordinary, an artless and short conversation with a girl. Inexhaustible as is the treasury of your majesty's bounties, I pray you to consider that it cannot be sufficient to your generosity; for if you recompense so slight a conversation by gifts so great, what will you be able to do for those who are ready to consecrate their entire obedience to your desires? How great soever may be the bounties I have received, the joy I feel in being loved by a king whom I adore, and to whom I would with pleasure make a sacrifice of my heart, if fortune had rendered it worthy of being offered to him, will ever be infinitely greater.

The warrant of maid of honour to the Queen induces me to think that your majesty has some regard for me. Since it gives me the means of seeing you oftener, and of assuring you by my own lips (which I shall do on the first opportunity) that I am,

Your majesty's very obliged and very obedient servant, without any reserve,

ANNE BOLEYN.

----◆----

Anne Boleyn's Last Letter to Henry VIII.

As a proper accompaniment to King Henry's love-letters, we put the last letter of Anne Boleyn to her royal husband, who had now ceased to be her lover, written from her prison in the Tower just before her execution. It is the letter of a woman without hope, who knows well the man to whom she writes, and is not afraid to speak clearly and bravely. There has been some slight doubt expressed as to the authenticity of this letter as well as of the foregoing; but it seems plain to me no one but Anne could have written it, and her allusion to Jane Seymour as "that party, for whose sake I am now as I am, whose name I could some while since have pointed unto; your Grace being not ignorant of my suspicions therein," is in true womanly spirit, and shows that there had been accusations on her part before the king began those counter-accusations which led to the unhappy queen's death.

THE TOWER, May 6, 1536.

SIR, — Your Grace's displeasure and my imprisonment are things so strange unto me, as what to write or what to excuse, I am altogether ignorant, whereas you send unto me (willing me to confess a truth, and so obtain your favour) by such an one whom you know to be mine ancient professed enemy. I no sooner received this message by him than I rightly conceived your meaning; and if, as you say, confessing a truth may procure my safety, I shall with all willingness and duty perform your command.

But let not your Grace ever imagine that your poor wife will ever be brought to acknowledge a fault where not so much as a thought thereof preceded. And, to speak truth, never prince had wife

more loyal in all duty and in all true affection
than you have ever found in Anne Boleyn, with
which name and place I could willingly have contented myself, if God and your Grace's pleasure
had been so pleased. Neither did I, at any time,
so far forget myself in my exaltation, or received
queenship, but that I always looked for such an
alteration as I now find; for the ground of my
preferment being on no surer foundation than
your Grace's fancy, the least alteration, I knew,
was sufficient to draw that fancy to some other
subject. You have chosen me from a low estate
to be your Queen and companion, far above my
desert and desire. If then you found me worthy
of such honour, good your Grace, let not any light
fancy, or bad counsel of mine enemies, withdraw
your princely favour from me; neither let that
stain, that unworthy stain of a disloyal heart
towards your good Grace, ever cast so foul a blot
on your most dutiful wife, and the infant princess,
your daughter. Try me, good King, but let me
have a lawful trial, and let not my sworn enemies
sit as my accusers and judges; yea, let me receive
an open trial, for my truth shall fear no open
shame; then shall you see, either mine innocency
cleared, your suspicion and conscience satisfied,
the ignominy and slander of the world stopped,

or my guilt openly declared. So that whatsoever God or you may determine of me, your Grace may be freed from an open censure, and mine offence being so lawfully proved, your Grace is at liberty, both before God and man, not only to execute worthy punishment on me as an unlawful wife, but to follow your affections already settled on that party, for whose sake I am now as I am, whose name I could some while since have pointed unto; your Grace being not ignorant of my suspicions therein.

But if you have already determined of me, and that not only my death, but an infamous slander, must bring you to the enjoying of your desired happiness, then I desire of God that he will pardon your great sin therein, and likewise mine enemies, the instruments thereof, and that he will not call you to a strict account for your unprincely and cruel usage of me, at his general judgment seat, where both you and myself must shortly appear, and in whose judgment I doubt not (whatsoever the world may think of me) mine innocence shall be openly known and sufficiently cleared. My last and only request shall be that myself may only bear the burden of your Grace's displeasure, and that it shall not touch the innocent souls of those poor gentlemen, who (as I understand) are likewise in strait imprisonment for my sake. If ever I have found favour in your sight, if ever the name of Anne Boleyn has been pleasant in your ears, then let me obtain this request; and I will so leave to trouble your Grace any further, with mine earnest prayers to the Trinity to have your Grace in his good keeping, and to direct you in all your actions. From my doleful prison in the Tower, this sixth of May.

Your most loyal and ever faithful wife,

ANNE BOLEYN.

Henry VIII. to Jane Seymour.

The following is the only other love-letter from Henry VIII. to any of his royal favourites, which is extant. This was written to Jane Seymour, Anne's successor to the dangerous position of queen, while Anne was in the Tower awaiting her death.

Jane Seymour died at the birth of her son the year following her marriage. The value of Henry's protestations of affection to any woman may be judged by this brief extract from old John Heywood's account of her death: —

"*News was sent to the king that her life was in great peril, nay, the issue was driven to so great an exigeance that either mother or child must necessarily perish; desiring the king to decide in so great an emergency. His answer was the mother should then die, for certain he was he could have more wives, but uncertain whether to have more children.*" On this the mother

was at once sacrificed to preserve the life of her son,
Prince Edward VI.

1536.

MY DEAR FRIEND AND MISTRESS, — The bearer
of these few lines from thy entirely devoted servant will deliver into thy fair hands a token of my
true affection for thee, hoping you will keep it forever in your sincere love for me. Advertising you
that there is a ballad made lately of great derision
against us, which if it go much abroad and is seen
by you, I pray you to pay no manner of regard to
it. I am not at present informed who is the setter
forth of this malignant writing, but if he is found
out he shall be straitly punished for it. For the
things ye lacked, I have minded my lord to supply
them to you as soon as he can buy them. Thus
hoping shortly to receive you in these arms, I end
for the present.

Your own loving servant and sovereign,

H., R.

———◆———

Katherine of Arragon to Henry VIII.

Of all the six women whom the royal Blue-beard took to
wife, it is probable that the only one who had any real affection for him was his first wife, KATHERINE OF ARRAGON.
This is her last letter to him, written after her divorce and

very shortly before her death. Shakespeare has given the substance of this letter in the last speeches of Katherine in *Henry VIII.*, Act IV. Scene 2.

1536 (?).

My Lord and dear Husband, — I commend me unto you. The hour of my death draweth fast on, and, my case being such, the tender love I owe you forceth me, with a few words, to put you in remembrance of the health and safeguard of your soul, which you ought to prefer before all worldly matters, and before the care and tendering of your own body, for the which you have cast me into many miseries and yourself into many cares. For my part I do pardon you all; yes, I do wish and devoutly pray God that he will also pardon you.

For the rest I commend unto you Mary, our daughter, beseeching you to be a good father unto her, as I heretofore desired. I entreat you also on behalf of my maids, to give them marriage-portions, which is not much, they being but three. For all my other servants I solicit a year's pay more than their due, lest they should be unprovided for.

Lastly, I do vow, mine eyes desire you above all things.

Katherine.

Katherine Parr to Henry VIII.

KATHERINE PARR, last queen of Henry VIII., had been previously twice married before she became queen-consort. She managed the king with great tact, although her life must have been a hard one. She was little else than a slavish nurse to the gouty person of the king, who had grown so obese that he was almost helpless. Katherine showed her satisfaction at escaping from such servitude by marrying Thomas Seymour, Lord High Admiral of England, as soon as the king's remains were comfortably deposited in the chapel choir at Windsor. This letter was probably written in 1544, while King Henry was absent upon his campaign in France.

1544 (?).

ALTHOUGH the distance of time and account of days neither is long nor many of your majesty's absence, yet the want of your presence, so much desired and beloved by me, maketh me that I cannot quietly pleasure in anything until I hear from your majesty. The time, therefore, seemeth to me very long, with a great desire to know how your highness hath done since your departing hence, whose prosperity and health I desire more than mine own. And whereas I know your majesty's absence is never without great need, yet love and affection compel me to desire your presence.

Again, the same zeal and affection forceth me

to be best content with that which is your will and pleasure. Thus love maketh me in all things to set apart mine own convenience and pleasure, and to embrace most joyfully his will and pleasure whom I love. God, the knower of secrets, can judge these words not to be written only with ink, but most truly impressed on the heart. Much more I omit, lest it be thought I go about to praise myself, or crave a thank; which thing to do I mind nothing less but a plain, simple relation of the love and zeal I bear your majesty, proceeding from the abundance of the heart. Wherein I must confess I desire no commendation, having such just occasion to do the same.

I make like account with your majesty as I do with God for his benefits and gifts heaped upon me daily, acknowledging myself a great debtor to him, not being able to recompense the least of his benefits; in which state I am certain and sure to die, yet I hope in his gracious acceptance of my good will. Even such confidence have I in your majesty's gentleness, knowing myself never to have done my duty as were requisite and meet for such a noble prince, at whose hands I have found and received so much love and goodness that with words I cannot express it.

Lest I should be too tedious to your majesty, I

finish this my scribbled letter, committing you to the governance of the Lord, with long and prosperous life here, and after this life to enjoy the kingdom of his elect.

From Greenwich, by your majesty's humble and obedient wife and servant,

KATERYN THE QUEEN.　K. P.

———◆———

Sir Christopher Hatton to Queen Elizabeth.

The following letter to Queen Elizabeth from one of her court favourites is among the very few love-letters to her which have come down to the present. As for the queen, she was probably too discreet to write letters of sentiment, as none such have been found from her hand.

CHRISTOPHER HATTON, who wrote the following, held the offices of Vice-Chamberlain and Lord Chancellor during the reign of Elizabeth, and for a time was a prime favourite. The queen had a number of odd pet-names for him; she called him her "sheep," her "lids" (eyelids), sometimes "her most sweet lids." He came to court quite an obscure gentleman, but he rose rapidly in favour, partly, no doubt, because, like Leicester and Raleigh, he was of handsome and graceful person. Robert Naunton, one of Elizabeth's counsellors, says: "The queen had much of her father in this, for (excepting some of her kindred, and some few that had handsome wits in their crooked bodies) she always took her a handsome person in the way of her choice; for the people have it to this day in proverb, 'King Harry loved a *man*.' One of his rivals says Hatton danced himself into favour by his grace in a galliard which he executed in some theatrical performance given before the queen; and as he was a gentleman who, besides the graces of his person and dancing, had the addition of strong and subtle capacity, he soon grew in favour and place."

June, 1573.

IF I could express my feelings of your gracious letters, I should utter unto you matter of strange effect. In reading of them, with my tears I blot them; in thinking of them I feel so great comfort that I find cause, as God knoweth, to thank you on my knees. Death had been much more to my advantage than to win health and life by so loathsome a pilgrimage. The time of two days hath drawn me further from you than ten, when I return, can lead me towards you. Madam, I find the greatest lack that ever poor wretch sustained. No death, no, not hell, no fear of death, shall ever win of me my consent so far to wrong myself again as to be absent from you one day. God grant my return. I will perform this vow. I lack that I live by. The more I find this lack, the further I go from you. Shame whippeth me forward. Shame take them that counselled me to it. The life (as you well remember) is too long that loathsomely lasteth. A true saying,

13

Madam; believe him that hath proved it. The great wisdom I find in your letters with your country counsels are very notable; but the last word is worth the Bible. Truth, truth, truth! Ever may it dwell with you. I will ever deserve it. My spirit and soul, I feel, agreeth with my body and life, that to serve you is a heaven, but to lack you is more than a hell's torment unto them. My heart is full of woe. Pardon, for God's sake, my tedious writing. It doth much diminish (for the time) my great griefs. I will wash away the faults of these letters with the drops from your poor " lids " and so enclose them. Would God I were with you but for one hour! My wits are overwrought with thoughts. I find myself amazed. Bear with me, my most sweet, dear lady. Passion overcometh me; I can write no more. Love me, for I love you. God, I beseech thee witness the same in the behalf of thy poor servant. Live forever! Shall I utter this familiar term (farewell?) yea, ten thousand thousand farewells. He speaketh it that most dearly loveth you. I hold you too long. Once again I crave pardon, and so bid your own poor " Lids " farewell.

Your bondsman everlastingly tied,

CH. HATTON.

The Earl of Essex to Queen Elizabeth.

The unfortunate EARL OF ESSEX, who was Queen Elizabeth's favourite in her last years, was more independent in spirit and less fulsome in his flattery to the queen than any of her previous favourites. Yet this letter, which was written when Essex was twenty-five and the queen sixty, is a very good specimen of the manner in which, during her life from twenty-five to seventy years of age, the queen was addressed by her courtiers.

No date.

MADAM, — The delights of this place cannot make me unmindful of one in whose sweet company I have joyed as much as the happiest man doth in his highest contentment; and if my horse could run as fast as my thoughts do fly, I would as often make mine eyes rich in beholding the treasure of my love, as my desires do triumph when I seem to myself in a strong imagination to conquer your resisting will. Noble and dear lady, though I be absent, let me in your favour be second unto none; and when I am at home, if I have no right to dwell chief in so excellent a place, yet I will usurp upon all the world. And so making myself as humble to do you service, as in my love I am ambitious, I wish your majesty all your happy desires.

Croydon, this Tuesday, going to be mad and make my horse tame. Of all the men the most devoted to your service.

Essex.

———◆———

Mary Queen of Scots to the Earl of Bothwell.

I quote the ensuing letter, claimed to have been written by Mary Queen of Scots to Bothwell, without any expression of opinion as to its authenticity. There is no fact alleged concerning that unfortunate and extraordinary queen and woman which has not been denied by one side or the other, on which are ranged her partisans and her accusers. Her accusers claim that there were found before her trial some authentic love-letters written by her to Bothwell, which prove that she was a party to the murder of her husband Lord Darnley, and to her abduction by Bothwell. When Bothwell fled from his enemies he left behind him in his haste a silver-gilt casket, which had been given to Mary by her first husband, Francis II. of France, containing twenty one letters and love-sonnets written by Mary to Bothwell. Seven of these letters, claimed by her enemies to be genuine, were printed by Buchanan in his History of Scotland. Her partisans vehemently deny their genuineness, and declare them forgeries.

Below is one of these disputed letters. It would appear to have been sent by the queen to Bothwell with some love-token, — a ring of black enamel containing an engraved stone, which Mary compares to her heart. The famous silver-gilt casket still exists, forever voiceless as to the nature of its contents three hundred years ago.

From Mary Queen of Scots to the Earl of Bothwell,
concerning certain Tokens that she sent him.

1567 (?).

MY LORD, — If the displeasure of your absence,
of your forgetfulness, the fear of danger promised
by every one to your so loved person, may give me
consolation, I leave it to you to judge, seeing the
mishap that my cruel lot and continual misadven-
ture has hitherto promised me following the misfortunes and fears as well of late, as of a long time
by past, the which you do know. But for all that
I will nowise accuse you, neither of your little remembrance, neither of your little care, and least
of all of your promise broken, or of the coldness
of your writing, since I am else so far made yours
that that which pleases you is acceptable to me;
and my thoughts are so willingly subdued unto
yours that I suppose that all that cometh of you
proceeds not of any the causes aforesaid, but
rather of such as be just and reasonable, and such
as I desire myself, which is the final order that
you promised to take for the surety and honour-
able service of the only supporter of my life. For
which alone I will preserve the same, and without
the which I desire nought but sudden death. And
to testify unto you how lowly I submit myself to

your commandments I have sent you of homage
by Pareis the ornament of the head which is the
chief guide of the other members. Inferring there-
by that by the seizing of you in the possession of
the spoil of which that is the principal, the rem-
nant cannot be but subject unto you, and with
consenting of the heart.

In place whereof, since I have else left it unto
you, I send unto you one sculpture of hard stone
coloured with black, engraved with tears and
bones. The stone I compare to my heart, that
as it is covered in one sure sepulture or harbour
of your commandments, and, above all, of your
name and memory, that are therein enclosed as is
my heart in this ring, never to come forth while
death grant unto you to one trophy of victory to
my bones, as the ring is filled, in sign you have
made one full conquest of me, of my heart, and
in that my bones are left unto you in remembrance of your victory and my acceptable love
and willingness, for to be better bestowed than I
merit. The annealing that is about is black,
which signifies the steadfastness of her that sends
the same. The tears are without number, so
are the fears to displease you, the tears for
your absence, the disdain that I cannot be in
outward effect yours, as I am without faintness

of heart and spirit, and of good reason, though my merits were much greater than that of the most profit that ever was, and such as I desire to be, and shall take pains in conditions to imitate, for to be bestowed worthily under your governance. My only wealth receive, therefore, in as good part the same, as I have received of your marriage in extreme joy, that which shall not part forth of my bosom till that marriage of our bodies be made in public, as a sign of all that I either hope or desire of bliss in this world.

Yet, my heart, fearing to displease you, as much in the reading hereof, as it delights me in the writing, I will make an end, after I have kissed your hand with as great affection as I pray God (oh, the only supporter of my life!) to give you long and blessed life, and to me your good favour, as the only good that I desire, and to the which I pretend. I have shown unto the bearer of this that which I have learned, knowing the credit that you give him; as she also doth, that will be forever unto you an humble and obedient lawful wife that forever dedicates unto you her heart, her body, without any change unto him I have made the possessor of my heart, of which you may hold you assured, that unto death shall no ways be changed, for evil nor good shall never make me go from it.

James I. to the Duke of Buckingham.

JAMES I., who was such a strange mixture of learning and foolishness, of weak cruelty and doting fondness, has left no letters to women to be placed in the catalogue of love-letters; but some of his letters to George Villiers, the Duke of Buckingham, whom he doted on with an affection which was more than womanish, are so much in the style of love-letters that one of them deserves a place in this collection. Buckingham seems to have been a lovable person, in spite of his faults. Clarendon says of him: "He was indeed an extraordinary person, and never any man in any age, nor, I believe, in any nation, rose, in so short a time, to so much greatness of honour, fame, and fortune, upon no other advantage or recommendation than the beauty and gracefulness of his person. I have not the least purpose of undervaluing his good parts, when I say that his first introduction into favour rose purely from the handsomeness of his person."

King James wrote to this favourite as his "sweet child," his "dear boy," and signed himself constantly "Your dear dad and gossip;" and Buckingham replied in much the same spirit, signing himself often his "dear dad's humble dog Steenie."

No date.

MY ONLY SWEET AND DEAR CHILD, — I am now so miserable a coward as I do nothing but weep and mourn; for I protest to God I rode this afternoon a great way in the park without speaking to anybody, and the tears trickling down my cheeks, as now they do, that I can scarcely see to write. But alas! what shall I do at our parting? The only small comfort that I have will be to pry into thy defects with the eye of an enemy, and of every mote to make a mountain, and so harden my heart against thy absence. But this little malice is like jealousy proceeding from a sweet root; but in one point it overcometh it, for as it proceeds from love, so it cannot but end in love.

Sweet heart! be earnest with Kate[1] to come and meet thee at New Hall within eight or ten days after this. Cast thee to be here to-morrow as near about two in the afternoon as thou canst, and come galloping hither. Remember thy picture, and suffer none of the council to come here. For God's sake! write not a word again, and let no creature see this letter. The Lord of heaven and earth bless thee, and my sweet daughter, and my dear little grandchild, and all thy blessed family, and send thee a happier turn, both now and thou knowest when, to thy dear dad and Christian gossip,

JAMES, R.

[1] The Duchess of Buckingham. See her letter to the Duke, p. 254.

Lady Arabella Stuart to her Husband.

Among royal ladies, the Lady ARABELLA STUART stands hardly second in misfortune to Lady Jane Grey, although her name is much less prominent in history. She was, like James I., descended from Margaret, the daughter of Henry VII., and so had some claim to the English succession after Elizabeth's death, which she seems never to have urged or to have wished urged in her favour. Yet it was through a pretended plot to put her on the throne that Raleigh was so long imprisoned in the Tower.

She was for years a source of alarm to James I., and was allowed neither liberty nor the pursuit of happiness during her ill-fated life, simply because she had the misfortune to be born near a throne. At length the poor lady added to her other misfortunes that of falling in love. Many matches had been proposed for her, but they were considered dangerous by some of the royal parties, and nipped in the bud, until William Seymour, afterwards Marquis of Hertford, boldly wooed her in person, and they were privately married. The marriage was kept hidden for a year, and then they were both imprisoned. Seymour was placed in the Tower for "marrying a member of the royal family without the king's leave." They managed to correspond for a time by letters, till this was discovered and stopped. Then the Lady Arabella fell ill, but in spite of illness made an attempt to escape with her husband, — an attempt which, just when it seemed ripe for success, was frustrated, and the poor lady was returned to prison. She sunk under these persecutions; meditated suicide; finally lost her reason, and sunk into a melancholy, in which she died. Seymour seems always to have cherished her memory; and years after, when his fortunes had brightened, his titles were granted him, and he had married a second time, he gave the daughter by this second marriage the name of *Arabella Stuart*.

This letter from the Lady Arabella is very pathetic, from its simplicity and womanly tenderness, in which there is mingled no resentment against her persecutors.

1610.

SIR, — I am exceeding sorry to hear you have not been well. I pray you let me know truly how you do, and what was the cause of it. I am not satisfied with the reason Smith gives of it; but if it be a cold, I will impute it to some sympathy betwixt us, having myself gotten a swollen cheek at the same time with a cold. For God's sake, let not your grief of mind work upon your body. You may see by me what inconveniences it will bring one to; and no fortune, I assure you, daunts me so much as that weakness of body I find in myself; for *si nous vivons l'age d'un veau*, as Marot says, we may, by God's grace, be happier than we look for, in being suffered to enjoy ourself with his majesty's favour. But if we be not able to live to it, I for my part shall think myself a pattern of misfortune in enjoying so great a blessing as you so little while. No separation but that deprives me of the comfort of you. *For wheresoever you be, or in what state soever you are, it suffi-*

ceth me you are mine. Rachel wept and would not be comforted, because her children were no more. And that, indeed, is the remediless sorrow, and none else! And therefore God bless us from that, and I will hope well of the rest, though I see no apparent hope. But I am sure God's book mentioneth many of his children in as great distress, that have done well after, even in this world. I do assure you nothing the State can do with me can trouble me so much as this news of your being ill doth; and you see when I am troubled I trouble you too, with tedious kindness; for so I think you will account so long a letter, yourself not having written to me this good while so much as how you do. But, sweet sir, I speak not this to trouble you with writing but when you please. Be well, and I shall account myself happy in being

Your faithful and loving wife,

ARB. S.

—◆—

Charles I. to Henrietta Maria.

The marriage of CHARLES I. with Henrietta Maria of France was doubtless an unusually happy state-marriage. They first saw each other at a court ball in Paris in 1623, when Charles, then Prince of Wales, was on his way to Spain, in company with the Duke of Buckingham and ·

Endymion Porter,[1] to visit the Spanish Infanta, who was the proposed wife of the prince. The Spanish match was abandoned, and two years later he married the French princess. History gives a very pretty picture of her coming to England: how she tried to kneel when presented to the king, how he prevented her by raising her in his arms, and how her arch coquetries won his heart. Whatever may be said of him as a king, he was a loyal husband and a tender father; and the domestic life of his court was in fine contrast to that of James I., who preceded, and of Charles II., who followed him. These two letters which follow were written when the king was holding his court at Oxford, during the Civil War, and after the queen had left England to seek an asylum in her native France.

OXFORD, Feb. 13, 1643.

DEAR HEART, — I never knew till now the good of ignorance ; for I did not know the danger that thou wert in by the storm [2] before I had assurance of thy happy escape, we having had a pleasing false report of thy safe landing at Newcastle, which thine of the 19th of January so confirmed us in that we at least were not undeceived of that hope till we knew certainly how great a danger thou hast passed, of which I shall not be out of apprehension until I may have the happiness of thy

[1] See letters of the Duchess of Buckingham and Endymion Porter, on pp. 254, 258.

[2] The storm took place on the queen's return from Holland, and she was obliged to put back for shelter.

company. For, indeed, I think it not the least of my misfortunes that for my sake thou hast run so much hazard; in which thou hast expressed so much love to me that I confess it is impossible to repay by anything I can do, much less by words. But my heart being full of affection of thee, admiration of thee, and impatient passion of gratitude to thee, I could not but say something, leaving the rest to be read by thee out of thine own noble heart. . . .

CHARLES, R.

The Same to the Same.

OXFORD, April 9, 1645.

DEAR HEART, — Though it be an uncomfortable thing to write by a slow messenger, yet all occasions of the which is now the only way of conversing with thee is so welcome to me as I shall be loth to lose any; but expect neither news nor public business from me by this way of conveyance. Yet, judging thee by myself, even these nothings will not be unwelcome to thee, though I should chide thee, which, if I could, I would do, for thy too sudden alarms.

I pray thee consider, since I love thee above all earthly things, and that my contentment is inseparably conjoined with thine, must not all my actions tend to serve and please thee? If thou knew what a life I lead, — I speak not in respect of common distractions, even in point of conversation, which in my mind is either the brief joy or vexation of one's life, — I dare say thou wouldst pity me ; for some are too wise, some too foolish, others too reserved, many too fantastic. When I know none better than [*here follow several names written in the cipher used by the king to the queen, which are therefore unintelligible*], thou mayest easily judge how thy conversation pleased me. I confess thy company has perhaps made me, in this, hard to be pleased, but not less to be pitied by thee, who art the only cure for this disease. The end of all this is to desire thee to comfort me as often as thou canst with thy letters ; and dost not thou think that to know particulars of thy health, and how thou spendest thy time, are pleasing subjects unto me when thou hast no other business to write of ?

Believe me, sweet heart, thy kindness is as necessary to comfort my heart as thy assistance is for my affairs.

CHARLES, R.

Oliver Cromwell to his Wife.

The following letters of OLIVER CROMWELL, written while he held as absolute sway over English lives and liberties as had ever been held by any of the royal house of Stuart, belong justly, I think, among the letters of royal persons. These letters, though brief, are characteristic, although perhaps they show the hard old Puritan in a light somewhat tenderer than that usually reflected on him by history.

For my beloved wife, ELIZABETH CROMWELL, at the Cockpit, these:

DUNBAR, Sept. 4, 1650.

MY DEAREST, — I have not leisure to write much; but I could chide thee that in many of thy letters thou writest to me that I should not be unmindful of thee and thy little ones. Truly, if I love you not too well, I think I err not on the other hand much. Thou art dearer to me than any creature; let that suffice.

The Lord hath showed us an exceeding mercy; who can tell how great it is! My weak faith hath been upheld. I have been in my inward man marvellously supported, though I assure thee I grow an old man and feel infirmities marvellously stealing upon me.[1] Would my corruptions did as

---

[1] He was then fifty-one.

fast decrease! Pray on my behalf in the latter respect. The particulars of our late success Harry Vane or Gilbert Pickering will impart to thee. My love to all dear friends.

I rest thine

OLIVER CROMWELL.

The Same to the Same.

For my beloved wife, ELIZABETH CROMWELL, at the Cockpit, these:

EDINBURGH, 3d May, 1651.

MY DEAREST, — I could not satisfy myself to omit this post, although I have not much to write; yet indeed I love to write to my dear, who is very much in my heart. It joys me to hear thy soul prospereth; the Lord increase his favours to thee more and more. The great good thy soul can wish is, that the Lord lift upon thee the light of his countenance, which is better than life. The Lord bless all thy good counsel and example to all those about thee, and hear all thy prayers and accept thee always.

I am glad to hear thy son and daughter are with thee.[1] I hope thou wilt have some good

---

[1] Richard Cromwell and wife.

14

opportunity of good advice to him.   Present my
duty to my mother, my love to all the family.
Still pray for thine

OLIVER CROMWELL.

——◆——

Charles II. to Catherine of Braganza.

This letter, written just before Catherine of Braganza
departed for England to be wedded to CHARLES II., is the
only love-letter I have found of the many which were
doubtless written by this royal Lothario.   This is rather
coldly, though courteously expressed, and may have struck
a chill to the heart of the unhappy princess, as a presage
of the neglect and wretchedness she was to suffer as his
wife.

LONDON, July 2, 1661.

MY LADY AND WIFE, — Already, at my request,
the good Count da Ponte has set off for Lisbon ;
for me, the signing of the marriage has been great
happiness, and there is about to be dispatched at
this time after him one of my servants, charged
with what would appear necessary ; whereby may
be declared, on my part, the inexpressible joy of
this felicitous conclusion, which, when received,
will hasten the coming of your majesty.

I am going to make a short progress into one
of my provinces ; in the meantime, whilst I go
from my most sovereign good, yet I do not com-

plain as to whither I go, seeking in vain tranquillity in my restlessness ; hoping to see the beloved person of your majesty in these kingdoms, already your own, and that with the same anxiety with which, after my long banishment, I desired to see myself within them, and my subjects, desiring also to behold me amongst them, having manifested their most ardent wishes for my return, well known to the world. The presence of your serenity is only wanting to unite us, under the protection of God, in the health and content I desire. I have recommended to the queen, our lady and mother, the business of the Count da Ponte, who, I must here avow, has served me in what I regard as the greatest good in this world, which cannot be mine less than it is that of your majesty ; likewise not forgetting the good Richard Russell, who laboured on his part to the same end.

The very faithful husband of your majesty, whose hand he kisses.

CHARLES, REX.

Letters of Queen Mary to King William.

The most genuinely womanly letters ever written by a lady of royal blood are the letters of QUEEN MARY II. of England to her husband and joint sovereign with her, William III. She writes in as simple and as housewifely a strain as if she were the wife of a citizen of simplest state in all England. It is easy to see who held the reins of government under the transparent pretence of their joint sovereignty. She writes him : " If I do anything you don't like, 't is my misfortune, not my fault; for I love you more than my own life, and desire only to please you."

When he is coming home from a journey she writes to beg, " that if possible I may come and meet you on the road, either where you dine, or anywhere else ; for I *do so long to see you* that I am sure, had *you* as much wish to see your poor wife again, you would propose it; but do as you please. I can say no more, but that I love you so much my love cannot increase, else I am sure it would." The following letters were all written to William during his campaign in Ireland, the first very near the date of the battle of the Boyne.

WHITEHALL, $\frac{2\ July}{22\ June}$, 1690, half 11 at Night.

THE news which is come to-night of the French fleet being upon the coast makes it necessary to write to you both ways ; and I, that you may see how matters stand in my heart, prepare a letter for each.

I think Lord Torrington has made no haste, and I cannot tell whether his being sick and staying for Lord Pembroke's regiment, will be a sufficient excuse ; but I will not take up your time with my reasonings. I shall only tell you that I am so little afraid that I begin to fear I have not sense enough to apprehend the danger; for whether it threatens Ireland or this place, to me 't is much at one as to the fear; for as much a coward as you think me, I fear more for your dear person than my poor carcass. I know who is most necessary in the world. What I fear most at present is not hearing from you. Love me, whatever happens, and be assured I am ever entirely yours till death.

———◆———

The Same to the Same.

WHITEHALL, July $\frac{26}{16}$, 1690.

LORD BÉLMONT torments me to write by his brother, which I do, though I have nothing to say more than I wrote last night. I am always glad of an opportunity of putting you in mind of me, though I hope 't is not absolutely necessary. All the news of the town yesterday was, that you were landed at Chester; pray God it were true, though I think there is no likelihood of it; yet I thought it pleasing, and the more because they have really said several things which have come to pass. I hope it may be so in this. I will not say more now, but that the Bishop of Salisbury has made a long thundering sermon this morning, which he has been with me to desire to print, which I could not refuse, though I should not have ordered it, for reasons which I told him. I am extreme impatient of hearing from you, which I hope in God will be before I sleep this night. If not, I think I shall not rest; but if I should meet with a disappointment of your not coming, I don't know what I shall do; for my desire of seeing you is equal to my love, which cannot end but with my life.

——◆——

The Same to the Same.

Whitehall, July $\frac{27}{17}$, 1690.

EVERY hour makes me more impatient to hear from you, and everything I hear stir, I think brings me a letter. I shall not go about to excuse myself. I know 't is a folly to a great degree to be so uneasy as I am at present, when I have no reason to apprehend any ill cause, but only might attribute your silence to your marching farther from Dublin, which makes the way longer. I have stayed until I am asleep, in hopes; but they are vain, and I must once more go to bed, and wish to be waked with a letter from you, — which I shall at last get, I hope. Till I know whether you come or no, I cannot resolve to write you all that has passed this day, till which time I thought you had given me wrong characters of men, but now I see they answer my expectation of being as little of a mind as of a body. Adieu! do but love me and I can bear anything.

———◆———

The Same to the Same.

These last two letters from Mary to her husband were written when she was impatiently awaiting his return from his Irish campaign, and was hurrying forward the repairs upon the palace at Kensington, which she was fitting up and making ready for his return.

WHITEHALL, $\frac{\text{Aug. 5}}{\text{July 26}}$, 1690.

LAST night I received yours from Benit-bridge, by which I find you designed to summon Waterford last Monday. I beseech God give you good success, and send you safe and quickly home. There was order taken yesterday in council for the proroguing the parliament for three weeks. I have been this evening at Kensington; for though I did believe you would not be willing to stay at Whitehall, yet I confess what you write me word makes me in a million of fears, especially since I must needs confess my fault, that I have not been pressing enough till it was too late. The outside of the house is the fiddling work, which takes up more time than one can imagine, and while the scaffolds are up the windows must be boarded up, but as soon as that is done your own apartment may be furnished; and though mine cannot possibly be ready yet awhile, I have found out a way if you please: which is, that I may make use of Lord Portland's, and he lie in some of the other rooms. We may lie in your chamber, and I go through the council-room down, or else dress me there. And as I suppose your business will bring you often to town, so I may take such times to see company here, and that part of the family which can't come there must stay here; for 't is no matter what inconveniences any else suffers for your dear sake; and this way I think the only one yourself will have will be my lying in your chamber, which you know I can make as easy to you as may be; our being there will certainly forward the work. I hope this letter will not come to your hands, but that you will be upon your way hither before this. My greatest fear is for your closets here; but if you will consider how much sooner you come back than one durst have hoped, you will forgive me, and I can't but be extreme glad to be so deceived. God in his mercy send us a happy meeting and a quick one, for which I am much more impatient than I can possibly express.

The Same to the Same.

WHITEHALL, Aug. $\frac{12}{22}$, 1690.

UNLESS I could express the joy I had at the thoughts of your coming, it will be in vain that I undertake telling you of the disappointment 't is to me that you do not come so soon. I began to be in great pain lest you had been in the storm a Thursday night, which I am told was great (though its being at the other side of the house hindered my hearing it), but was soon delivered by your letter of the 29th from Ch. I confess I deserve such a stop to my joy, since may be it was too great; and I am not thankful enough to God, and we are all apt to be too vain upon so quick a success. But I have mortification enough to think your dear person may be again exposed at the passage of the Shannon as it was at that of the Boyne. This is what goes to my heart; but yet I see the reasons for it so good that I will not murmur, for certainly your glory would be the greater to terminate the war this summer, and the people here much better pleased than if they must furnish next year for the same thing again. Upon these considerations I ought to be satisfied, and I will endeavour as much as may be to submit to the will of God and your judgment; but you must forgive a poor wife, who loves you so dearly, if I can't do it with dry eyes. Yet, since it hath pleased God so wonderfully to preserve you all your life, and so miraculously now, I need not doubt but he will still preserve you; yet let me beg you not to expose yourself unnecessarily, — that will be too much tempting that Providence which I hope will still watch over you. Mr. Russel is gone down to the fleet last Thursday, to hasten as much as may be all things there, and will be back a Monday, when there is a great council appointed. I don't doubt but this Commission will find many obstacles; and this naming Killigrew among such as don't like him will be called in question, as well as the other two, and I shall hear again that 't is a thing agreed among two or three. I will not write now, no more than I used to do, what others can; and indeed I am fit for nothing this day, my heart is so oppressed. I don't know what to do. I have been at Kensington for some hours quiet, to-morrow being the first Sunday of the month, and have made use of Lord Portland's closet, as I told you in my last I would.

The house would have been ready by Tuesday night, and I hope will be in better order now;

at least, it shall not be my fault if 't is not. I shall be very impatient to hear again from you, till when I shall be in perpetual pain and trouble; which I think you can't wonder at, knowing that you are dearer to me than life.

———◆———

Prince Albert to Queen Victoria.

This letter from ALBERT, Prince-Consort to Queen Victoria, closes this collection of royal letters. It was written by Prince Albert just after his parting from the queen for a visit to Germany, his first absence from her after their marriage.

"PRINCESS ALICE," IN DOVER HARBOUR,
March 28, 1844.

MY OWN DARLING, — We got over our journey thus far rapidly and well, but the tide has been so unmannerly as to be an hour later than the calculated time, so that I cannot sail before three. Nevertheless Smithett promises to deposit me at Ostend by half past seven. I have been here about an hour, and regret the lost time I might have spent with you. Poor child! you will, while I write, be getting ready for luncheon, and will find a place vacant where I sat yesterday. In your heart, however, I hope my place will not be vacant. I, at least, have you on board with me in spirit.

I reiterate my entreaty, "bear up," and do not give way to low spirits, but try to occupy yourself as much as possible. You are even now half a day nearer to seeing me again; by the time you get this letter it will be a whole day; thirteen more, and I am again within your arms.

The railroad is wonderful, especially that part of it between this and Folkestone. I have gone through part of the fortifications with some of the commanding officers, and am now writing in a handsome cabin of the "Princess Alice." They are on the point of raising the anchor, which makes a hideous clatter.

Our caravan is complete. The sun shines brightly, and the sea is calm. To-morrow Seymour will bring you further news of me.

Your most devoted
ALBERT.

PART III.

LETTERS OF STATESMEN, MILITARY MEN, AND MEN OF AFFAIRS.

I assert, then, that although all the gods are immortally happy, Love, if I dare trust my voice to express so awful a truth, is the happiest and most excellent and most beautiful of all. — PLATO.

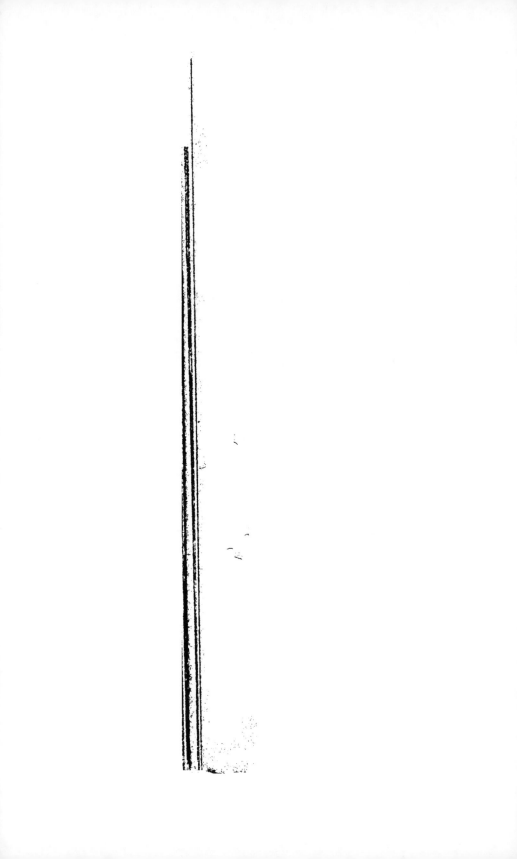

PART III.

LETTERS OF STATESMEN, MILITARY MEN, AND MEN OF AFFAIRS.

The Paston Letters.[1]

ONE of the most interesting collections of old letters which has come down to us from the past is that of the Paston family, who were people of consequence in the fifteenth century. Their domestic correspondence, which was carefully preserved, throws a vivid light on the social and family life of the time. The head of the family about the middle of the century was JOHN PASTON, whose wife, MARGARET, writes a large number of the letters in the collection.

She was an affectionate wife as well as a true helpmeet. The following is one of her letters written in their early married life, when her husband had been ill away from home, in his lodgings in the Temple in London. Every woman will appreciate the tenderness with which she writes him, that she would rather he would have been at home, if he could have had there as good care as she knows he had received in London, than have had a new gown, even though it were of scarlet.

---

[1] The spelling, and occasionally an old English word, of the Paston letters here transcribed, have been modernized, in order that they might be more readily understood by the general reader.

Margaret Paston to her Husband.

To my right worshipful husband, JOHN PASTON, dwelling at the Inner Temple in London, in haste.

OXNEAD, 28 Sept., 1443.

RIGHT WORSHIPFUL HUSBAND, — I recommend me to you, desiring heartily to hear of your welfare, thanking God of your mending of the great disease ye have had; and I thank you for the letter that ye sent me, for by my troth my mother and I were not in heart's ease from the time that we wist of your sickness till we wist verily of your mending. My mother behested another image of wax of the weight of you, to Our Lady of Walsingham, and she sent four nobles to the four orders of friars at Norwich to pray for you, and I have behested to go on a pilgrimage to Walsingham and to St. Leonard's for you. By my troth, I had never so heavy a season as I had from the time I wist of your sickness till I wist of your mending; and since, my heart is not in great ease nor I wot shall be till I wot that ye be very hale. Your father and mine was this day sevennight at Bekeleys for a matter for the prior of Bronholme, and he lay at Gerlyston that night and was there till IX. of the clock and the other day. And I sent thither for a gown, and my mother said that

I should have then, till I be there anon, and so they could none get.

My father Garneys sent me word that he should be here next week, and my uncle also, and hunt here with their hawks, and they should take me home with them ; and so, God help me, I shall excuse me of my going thither if I may, for I suppose that I shall readilier have tidings from you here than I should have there. . . . I pray you heartily that ye will vouchsafe to send me a letter as hastily as ye may, if writing be no disease to you ; and that ye will vouchsafe to send me word how your sore doeth. If I might have had my will I should have seen you ere this time. I would ye were at home — if it were your ease, and your sore might have been as well looked after here as there it has been — now, liever than a gown, though it were of scarlet. I pray you if your sore be healed, and so that ye may endure to ride, that ye will ask leave, and come home, when the horse shall be sent back again ; for I hope ye could be kept as tenderly here as ye have been in London. I may not liever have to do written a quarter as much as I should say to you if I might but speak to you. I shall send another letter as hastily as I may. I thank you that you would vouchsafe to remember my girdle, and that ye would write to me at the time, for I suppose that writing was not easy to you. Almighty God have you in his keeping, and send you health.

Written at Oxnead, in right great haste on St. Michael's Eve.

Yours,

M. Paston.

My mother greets you well, and sendeth you God's blessing and hers; and she prayeth you, and I pray you also, that ye be well dieted of meat and drink, for that is the greatest hope ye have now to your health-ward. Your son fareth well, blessed be God!

————◆————

Sir John Paston to Anne Haute.

Madame Margaret Paston, who wrote the above letter, had several children, among them two sons named John, and a daughter named for herself, and familiarly known as "Margery." The oldest son, John, was made a knight when twenty-one years old, which made him a very desirable match for the young ladies of the time. He seems to have been difficult to suit and to have paid his addresses to several without result, for he died a bachelor in 1487. This letter was written by him to a lady of French birth but English family, residing in Calais, with whom for some years he seems to have kept up a desultory courtship.

21 July, 1468.

SINCE it is so that I may not, as oft as I would, be where I might do my message myself, mine own fair mistress Anne, I pray you to accept this billet from my messenger to recommend me to you in my most faithful wise, as he that fainest of all others desireth to know of your welfare, which I pray God increase to your most pleasure.

And, Mistress, though so be that I have as yet given you but little cause to remember me, for lack of acquaintance, I beseech you let me not be forgot when you reckon up all your servants, to set me among the number.

I pray you, Mistress Anne, for that service that I owe you, that in as short time as ye goodly may, that I might be ascertained of your intent and of your best friends in such matters as I have broken to you of, which both your and mine right trusty friends John Lee, or else my mistress his wife, promised before you and me, at our first and last being together, that as soon as they, or either of them, knew your intent and your friend's, they should send me word. And if they do so I trust soon after to see you. And now farewell, mine own fair lady, and God give you good rest, for in faith I trow ye be in bed. Written on my way homeward, on St. Mary Magdalene's day at midnight.

Your own

JOHN PASTON.

P. S. Mistress Anne, I am proud that ye can read English. Wherefore I pray you acquaint you with this my rude hand, for my purpose is ye should be more acquainted with it, or else it shall be against my will ; but yet, and when ye have read this billet, I pray you burn it, or keep it secret to yourself, as my faithful trust is in you.

———◆———

Margery Brews to John Paston.

After the death of the first Sir John Paston, in 1487, his brother, the second John, succeeded him in the title and became the chief personage in- the family. He seems to have been also difficult to suit in a wife, and was several years in search of one. Before the elder Sir John's death, this younger brother was constantly seeking the inter- cession and counsel of the head of the family regarding his marriage, often having two or three matches under con- sideration at about the same time. At last in 1477 he met his fate in the person of Mistress MARGERY BREWS, who seems to have had the requisite decision of character to bring him to the point. John, the younger, had consulted the parents of Margery about the portion they proposed

to give with their daughter (a very important consideration with him, by the way), and the cautious father of the
girl had reserved his decision about the money settlement.
Dame Elizabeth Brews, the mother, invited young John to
their house at Topcroft, to meet Margery, but cautioned
him on no account to reveal to her that he stood in the position of a suitor till the money matter was settled. But it
seems that John had neglected this caution, and only a
little after his visit, just before Valentine's day, 1477, the
mother writes to John in this wise : —

"You promised me not to break the matter to Margery
until such time as ye and I were at point. But ye have
made her such an advocate for you that I may never have
rest, day nor night, for her calling and crying me to bring
the said matter to effect.

"Now, cousin, upon Friday is St. Valentine's day, when
every bird chooseth him a mate; and if it like you to come
Thursday at night and stay here till Monday, I trust to
God ye shall speak to my husband, and I shall pray ye
may bring the matter to a conclusion."

In spite of this there must still have been some holding
off about money matters, on the part of father Brews, and
he was evidently unwilling to give as much dowry with
his daughter as John desired, for the young lady herself
felt obliged to follow up her mother's letter with these two
ardent, yet business-like epistles. It is a comfortable
thing to learn that these letters ended the affair, and the
wavering John, who had one or two other ladies in his
mind, settled it in favour of Margery, and she became his
wife that year. The attempts at poetry in Mistress Margery's valentine may serve as a model for modern efforts
in that line.

Margery Brews to John Paston.

Unto my right well-beloved Valentine, JOHN PASTON, Esq., be this billet delivered.

TOPCROFT, Feb., 1477.

RIGHT reverend and worshipful and my right well-beloved Valentine, I recommend me unto you, full heartily desiring to hear of your welfare, which I beseech Almighty God long to preserve unto his pleasure and your heart's desire. And if it please you to hear of *my* welfare, I am not in good health of body or of heart, nor shall be till I hear from you.

> For there wots no creature what pain I endure,
> And for to be deed, I dare not it discure [discover].

And my lady, my mother, has laboured the matter to my father full diligently, but she can no more get than ye know of, for the which God knoweth I am full sorry. But if that ye love me, as I trust verily that ye do, ye will not leave me therefor; for if *ye* had not half the livelihood that ye have, for to do the greatest labour that any woman alive might, I would not forsake *you*.

And if ye command me to keep true wherever I go,
I wis I will do all my might you to love and never no mo';
And if my friends say that I do amiss,
They shall not prevent me so for to do.

My heart me bids evermore to love you
Truly over all earthly thing,
And if they be never so wroth
I trust it shall be better in time coming.

No more to you at this time, but the Holy
Trinity have you in his keeping. And I beseech
you that this billet be not seen of no earthly creature save only yourself, &c.

And this letter was indite at Topcroft with full
heavy heart

By your own

MARGERY BREWS.

—◆—

The Same to the Same.

To my right well-beloved cousin, JOHN PASTON, Esq., be
this letter delivered.

FEBRUARY, 1477.

RIGHT worshipful and well-beloved Valentine,
in my most humble wise I recommend me to
you, &c. And heartily I thank you for the letter which ye sent me by John Bekarton, whereby
I understand and know that ye be purposing
to come to Topcroft in short time, and without any errand or matter, but only to have a
conclusion of the matter between my father and
you. I would be most glad of any creature alive,
so that this matter might grow to effect. And
there as ye say, and ye come and find the matter

no more towards you than ye did aforetime, ye would no more put my father and my lady, my mother, to no cost nor business for that cause, a good while after, which causeth mine heart to be right heavy; and if that ye come, and the matter come to no result, then should I be much *more* sorry and full of heaviness.

And as for myself I have done and understand in the matter all that I can or may, as God knoweth, and I let you plainly understand that my father will no more money part withal in that behalf but 500*l.* and 50*m.*, which is right far from the accomplishment of your desire.

Wherefore, if that ye could be content with that good and my poor person, I would be the merriest maiden on ground, and if ye think not yourself satisfied, or that ye might have much more good, as I have understood by you before, good, true, and loving Valentine, that ye take no such labour upon ye as to come more for that matter; but let it pass, and never more be spoken of as I may be your true lover and bedwoman during my life.

No more to you at this time, but Almighty Jesus preserve you, both body and soul!

By your Valentine,

MARGERY BREWS.

Richard Calle to Margery Paston.

There is so little sentiment to be found in the wooing of the two Sir Johns, that it is refreshing to find it green and flourishing in the heart of Margery Paston, the sister of these two gentlemen. That Margery felt a true affection is proved by the fact that she kept loyal through the course of a love that ran anything but smooth.

It seems that Sir John, the elder brother, had a bailiff in charge of his estates named Richard Calle, who was a very valuable man of business in the family, a young man, and one who by his letters seems quite equal, if not superior in mind, to the gentlemen of the Paston family. On him Lady Margery set her heart, and being, by all evidence, a young woman of strong will, "where she had set her heart, there it must abide." The wroth and opposition of her family were extreme, and when we consider what an unusual thing it was in the fifteenth century for a young woman to breast the opposition of all her kinsfolk, we must have both sympathy and admiration for her as a brave and loyal girl. Before her family had quite found out the matter she had entered into a solemn troth-plight with Richard, — a plight the Church considered sacred, and which, if certain words were uttered, even her kinsfolk would not dare to annul, as they were binding in the eyes of the Church. If she had said this thing, her friends would not (as Richard Calle writes her), "if ye tell them solemnly the truth, damn their souls for us," as they would be in danger of doing if they annulled a troth-plight. So Margery was carried before the Bishop of Norwich, who was the nearest dignitary of the Church, to be examined as to the validity of her contract. The Bishop began by reminding her of her high birth and the friends she had and would have if she allowed herself to be ruled by them, and then asked her if she had said words to Calle that meant matrimony. Then Margery stood up bravely and repeated her words, and said, "if these words were not sure, she would make them still surer ere she went home, for she knew in her conscience she was bound, whatever the words she said." On which her mother and brothers waxed so much more wroth that they refused even to let her enter their doors while the Bishop was deciding the case, and the reverend judge was obliged to find a shelter in Norwich for her. He finally decided in favour of the lovers, and she became Mistress Richard Calle, who still continued his services in the family as bailiff, being too valuable a man to part with, although he seems never to have been received as a member of the family. Thus ends this romance of 1469, and here is one of its remains in the letter of Richard to Margery, written before she had her trial of love before the good Bishop of Norwich. Of Margery's letters we have none preserved; very likely they were destroyed by her family.

1469 (May?).

MINE own lady and mistress, and before God very true wife, I with heart full sorrowful recommend me to you, as he that cannot be merry, nor nought shall be till it is otherwise with us than it is yet, for this life that we lead now is neither pleasure to God nor to the world, considering the great bond of matrimony that is betwixt us, and also the great love that hath been and, as I trust, is yet betwixt us, and on my part never greater. Where-

fore I beseech Almighty God comfort us as soon
as it pleases him, for we that ought of very right
to be most together are most asunder : meseemeth
it is a thousand years ago since I spake with you.
I had liever than all the good in the world I might
be with you. Alas, alas, good lady, full little remember they what they do that keep us asunder ;
four times in the year are they cursed that hinder
matrimony ; it causeth many men to deem they
have large conscience in other matters as well as
herein. But what lady suffers as ye have done?
Make ye as merry as ye can, for I wis, lady, at
the long way, God will of his right wiseness help
his servants that mean truly and would live according to his laws.

I understand, lady, that ye have made as much
sorrow for me as any gentlewoman hath had in the
world. Would God all the sorrow ye have had,
had rested upon me, so that ye had been dis-
charged of it, for I wis, dear lady, it is to me a
death that ye be treated otherwise than ye ought to
be. This is a painful life that we lead. I cannot
live thus without it be a great displeasure to God.

Also like you to wit that I sent you a letter by
my lad, from London, and he told me that he
might not speak with you, there was made so
great await upon him and upon you both. He

told me John Thresher came to him in your name,
and said that ye sent him to my lad for a ring or
a token which I should have sent you, but he
trusted him not; he would not deliver him none.
After that he brought him a ring saying that ye
sent it him, commanding him that he should deliver the letter or token to him, which I conceive
was not by your sending; it was by my mistress's
and Sir James's advice. Alas! what mean they?
I suppose they deem we be not ensured together,
and if they do so I marvel, for then they are not
well advised, remembering the plainness that I
break to my mistress in the beginning, and I suppose by you both, and ye did as ye ought to do
of very right; and if you have done the contrary,
as I am informed ye have done, ye did neither
conscientiously nor to the pleasure of God, unless
ye did it for fear, and for the time to please such
as were at that time about you, and if ye so did
it for this service it was for a reasonable cause,
considering the great and unbearable calling upon
that ye had, and many an untrue tale was told you
of me, which God knows I was never guilty of.

My lad told me that my mistress, your mother,
asked him if he had brought any letter to you; and
many other things she bear him on hand, and
among all other, at the last she said to him that I

would not make her acquainted with the beginning, but she supposed I would at the ending; and as to that, God knows she knew first of me and none other. I wot not what her mistressbip meant; for, by my troth, there is no gentlewoman alive that my heart tendereth more than it doth her, nor is loather to displease, saving only your person, which of very right I ought to tender and love best, for I am bound thereto by the law of God, and so will do while I live, whatsoever befalls. I suppose, and ye tell them solemnly the truth, they will not damn their souls for us; though I tell them the truth, they will not believe me as well as they will do you; and therefore, good lady, at the reverence of God, be plain to them and tell them the truth, and if they will in no wise agree thereto, betwixt God, the Devil, and them be it; and that peril that we should be in, I beseech God it may lie upon them and not upon us. . . .

Madame, I am afraid to write you, for I understand ye have showed the letters that I have sent you before this time, but I pray you let no creature see this letter. As soon as ye have read it, let it be burnt, for I would no man should see it in no wise. Ye had no writing from me this two years, nor I would not send ye no more; therefore I remit all this matter to your wisdom.

Almighty Jesu preserve, keep, and give you your heart's desire, which I wot well would be to God's pleasure.

This letter was written with as great pain as ever wrote I thing in my life; for in good faith I have been right sick, and yet am not very well at ease. God amend it, &c.

Roger Ascham to his Wife Margaret, in Consolation for the Death of their Son, Sturm Ascham.

The following letter was written by ROGER ASCHAM, the famous schoolmaster of the sixteenth century. He was the teacher of Queen Elizabeth in her girlhood, and of Lady Jane Grey; and these two princesses seem to have been favourite pupils of his, for he cannot speak too highly in praise of their learning and studiousness.

His marriage, which took place rather late in life, when he was nearly forty, seems to have been a very happy one. At the time of his marriage he wrote thus to his friend John Sturm :—

" You wish to know about my wife. In face she is like her aunt, the wife of Sir R. Walop. She is just such a wife as John Sturm would desire for his friend Roger Ascham. Her name is Margaret; our wedding-day was the 1st of June, 1554, if there be anything lucky in that name or that day."

NOVEMBER, 1568.

MINE OWN GOOD MARGARET, — The more I think on your sweet babe, as I do many times, both day and night, the greater cause I always find of giving thanks continually to God for his singular goodness bestowed at this time upon the child, yourself, and me, even because it has rather pleased him to take the child to himself in heaven than to leave it here with us still on earth. When I mused on the matter as nature, flesh, and fatherly fantasy did carry me, I found nothing but sorrows and care, which did very much vex and trouble me; but at last, forsaking these worldly thoughts, and referring me wholly to the will and order of God in the matter, I found such a change, such a cause of joy, such a plenty of God's grace towards the child, and of his goodness towards you and me, as neither my heart can comprehend nor yet my tongue express the twentieth part thereof.

Nevertheless, because God and good-will hath so joined me and you together as we must not only be the one a comfort to the other in sorrow, but also partakers together in any joy, I could not but declare unto you what just cause I think we both have of comfort and gladness, by that God hath so graciously dealt with us as he hath. My first step from care to comfort was this: I thought God had done his will with our child, and because God by his wisdom knoweth what is best,

and by his goodness will do best, I was by and
by fully persuaded the best that can be is done
with our sweet child; but seeing God's wisdom is
unsearchable with any man's heart, and his goodness unspeakable with any man's tongue, I will
come down from such high thoughts and talk more
sensibly with you, and lay before you such matter
as may be both a full comfort for our cares past,
and also a just cause of rejoicing as long as we
live.   You well remember our continual wish and
desire, our nightly prayer together, that God would
vouchsafe to us to increase the number of the
world; we wished that nature should beautifully
perform the work by us; we did talk together how
to bring up our child in learning and virtue; we
had care to provide for it, so as honest fortune
should favour and follow it.   And see, sweet wife,
how mercifully God hath dealt with us in all
points; for what wish could desire, what prayer
could crave, what nature could perform, what virtue could deserve, what fortune could perform,
both we have received and our child doth enjoy already.   And because our desire (thanked be God)
was always joined with honesty and our prayers
mingled with fear, the will and pleasure of God
hath given us more than we wished, and that is
better for us now than we could hope to think

upon; but you desire to hear and know how, marry, even thus we desired to be made vessels to increase the earth, and God hath made us vessels to increase heaven, which is the greatest honour to man, the greatest joy to heaven, the greatest spite to the devil, the greatest sorrow to hell, that any man can imagine. Secondarily, when nature had performed what she would, grace stepped forth and took our child from nature, as where it could not creep in earth by nature, it was straightway able to soar to heaven by grace. It could not then speak by nature, and now it does praise God by grace; it could not then comfort the sick and careful mother by nature, and now, through prayer, is able to help father and mother by grace; and yet, thanked be nature, that hath done all she could do, and blessed be grace, that hath done more and better than we would wish she should have done. Peradventure you do wish that nature had kept it from death a little longer; yea, but grace has carried it where now no sickness can follow nor any death hereafter meddle with it; and instead of a short life with troubles on earth, it doth live a life that shall never end, with all manner of joys in heaven.

And now, Margaret, go to, I pray you, and tell

16

me as you think, do you love your sweet babe so little, do you envy his happy state so much, yea, once to wish that nature should have followed your pleasure in keeping your child in this miserable world, than that grace should have purchased such profit for your child as bringing him to felicity in heaven? Thirdly, you may say to me, — if the child had lived in this world, it might have come to such goodness by grace and virtue as might have turned to great comfort to us, to good service to our country, and served to have deserved as high a place in heaven as he doth now. To this in short, I answer, ought we not in all things to submit to God's good will and pleasure, and thereafter to rule our affections, which I doubt not but you will endeavour to do. And therefore I will say no more, but with all comfort to you here, and a blessing hereafter, which I doubt not but is prepared for you,

Your dearly loving husband,

ROGER ASCHAM.

To my dear wife, MARGARET ASCHAM, these.

Sir William St. Lo to his Wife.

The Countess of Shrewsbury was one of the most remarkable women of the reign of Queen Elizabeth; beautiful in person, though masculine in character, and by all evidence utterly selfish and without heart. Yet her fascination helped her to four husbands; each of whom seems to have been equally in love with her, and each of whom she ruled with imperious sway. This letter from her third husband, WILLIAM ST. Lo, a bluff soldier of Elizabeth's guard, was written while he was stationed at the queen's palace in Windsor.

4 SEPTEMBER (about 1560?).

MY OWN, — More dearer to me than I am to myself, thou shalt understand that it is no small fear nor grief to me of thy well-doing than I should presently see what I dowgst, not only for that my continual nightly dreams beside my absence have troubled me, but also chiefly that Hugh Alsop cannot certify me in what estate thou nor thine is, whom I tender more than I do William St. Lo. Therefore I pray thee, as thou dost love me, let me shortly hear from thee, for the quieting of my unquieted mind, how thine own sweet self with all thine doeth, trusting shortly I may be among you. All my friends here saluteth thee. Harry Skipwith desired me to make thee and none other privy that he is sure of Mistress Nell, with whom he is by this time. He hath sent ten thousand thanks unto thyself for the same. She hath opened all her heart unto him.

To-morrow, Sir Richard Sackville and I ride to London together; upon Saturday next we return hither again.   The Queen [*Elizabeth*] yesterday her own self riding upon the way craved my horse, unto whom I gave him, receiving openly for the same many goodly words.

Thus wishing myself with thyself, I bid thee, my own good servant and chief overseer of my works, most heartily farewell.   From thine who is wholly and only thine, yea, and for all thine while life lasteth.

From Windsor, the 4th of September, by thy right worshipful master and most honest husband,

MASTER SIR WILLIAM ST. LO., ESQ.

———◆———

Earl of Shrewsbury to the Countess.

After the death of William St. Lo his lady married GEORGE TALBOT, Earl of Shrewsbury, who was as much enamoured of her as any of the three husbands who had preceded him.   As in her previous marriages, she schemed very cleverly to get the lion's share of the property into her hands and a controlling influence over his affairs.   But in some of her scheming she overreached herself.   Not long after her marriage with the Earl, Mary Queen of Scots threw herself upon the protection of Elizabeth, "her cousin and sister-queen."   As soon as Mary's coming to England was made certain, the Countess of Shrewsbury began to seek for her husband the dangerous honour of custodian to the person of the Scottish queen.   In this she succeeded.

Elizabeth placed her charge in the keeping of the Earl and Countess, and their castle was turned, in a manner, into a prison to hold the royal guest. It was not long after, that trouble began in the family of the Earl of Shrewsbury. Whether Mary Stuart used her fascination to excite the Earl's compassion and alleviate her captivity, is not certain, though not unlikely. It is certain that for once the managing Countess found her rival, if not her match. She could not conceal her discontent with the affairs in her household, and when Queen Elizabeth one day inquired how her prisoner fared, she made answer: "She cannot fare *ill* while she is with my husband; and I begin to grow jealous, they are so great together."

Queen Mary herself writes to one of her friends in France: "I have twice informed you minutely of the scandalous reports which have been circulated of my intimacy with the Earl of Shrewsbury. These have originated with *no one but his good lady herself.* If the Queen of England doth not have this calumny cleared up, I shall be obliged openly to attack the Countess of Shrewsbury herself."

It was not long after this that Elizabeth compelled the Earl to relinquish his charge, but not before he and his Countess had fallen into such disagreement as was never wholly removed, although at last a peace was patched up between them. The Earl died some time before his wife, who spent her latest days in bickering and contentions with different members of her family, and in building and repairing the castles in her possession, — an occupation which seemed to gratify the ambition of her restless old age.

The following letters were written to her by the Earl in the days of their early wedded life before she had begun to be jealous of Queen Mary, at the time even when she was planning to secure the office of custodian to the queen for her husband.

HAMPTON COURT, 1568.

MY DEAR ONE, — Having received a letter of the 1st of December, which came in very good time, else had I sent one of the few remaining with me, to have brought me word of your health, which I doubted of, for that I heard not from you of all this time till now, which drove me in the dumps, but now relieved again by your writing unto me.

I thank you, sweet one, for your puddings and venison. The puddings I have disposed in this wise: dozen to my Lady Cobham, and as many to my Lady Stuard and unto my Lady of Leicester, and the rest I have reserved to myself to eat in my chamber. The venison is yet in London, but I have sent for it thither.

I perceive Ned Talbot hath been sick, and now past danger. I thank God I have such a one that is so careful over me and mine. God send me soon home to possess my greatest joy. If you think that is *you*, you are not deceived.

. . . I live in hope to be with you before you can return answer again. You shall under-stand that this present Monday, in the morn-

ing, finding the queen in the garden at good
leisure, I gave her majesty thanks that she had
so little regard to the clamorous people of Bolsor
in my absence! She declared unto me what evil
speech had been said against me, and my nearness
and state in housekeeping, and as much as was
told her which she nowise believed, with as good
words from her as I could wish, declaring that·ere
it were long I should well perceive she did trust
me as she did few. She would not tell me
wherein, but I doubt it was about the custody of
the Queen of Scots. . . . I think before Sunday
these matters will come to some pass that we shall
know how long our abode shall be, but howsoever
it falls out I will not fail but be with you at Christmas, or else you shall come to me.

The plague is dispersed far abroad in London,
so the queen keeps her Christmas here and goeth
not to Greenwich, as it was meant. My Lady
Cobham wishes your presence here ; she loves you
well. I tell her I have cause to love her best for
that she wished me well speed with you, and I did.
*And as the pen writes, so the heart thinks, that of all
earthly joys I thank God chiefest for you, for with
you I have joys and contentation of mind, and without you death is more pleasant to me than life if I
thought I should be long from you, and therefore,*

good wife, do as I will do, hope shortly of our meeting, and farewell, dear, sweet one!

From Hampton Court this Monday at midnight, for it is every night so late before I go to bed, being at play in the privy chamber at Primers, where I have lost almost one hundred pounds and lacked my sleep besides.

Your faithful husband till death,

G. SHREWSBURY.

The Same to the Same.

MY DEAR ONE, — Of all joys I have under God the greatest is yourself. To think I possess one so faithful and one that I know loves me so dearly, is all, and the greatest comfort, that this earth can give. Therefore, God give me grace to be thankful to him for his good showed upon me a vile sinner. [*Part of the letter here is effaced and the meaning obscure.*]

I thank you, sweet heart, that you are so ready to come when I will; therefore, dear heart, send me word how I might send for you, and till I may have your company I shall think it long, my only joy, and therefore appoint a day, and in the meantime I shall content me with your will, and long daily for your coming.

I your letters con very well, and I like them so well they could not be amended, and I have sent them up to Gilbert. I have written him how happy he is to have such a mother as you are. Farewell, my only joy. This Tuesday eve.

Your faithful one,

To my Wife. Shrewsbury.

------◆------

Walter Raleigh to his Wife.

The following beautiful letter was written by Sir Walter Raleigh to his wife after his trial for treason and condemnation to death in 1603. His sentence was afterwards reprieved and he was committed to imprisonment in the Tower, where he remained more than twelve years, his captivity during much of that time softened by the society and affection of his wife. During his imprisonment he wrote his *History of the World,* and he occupied himself also in experiments in chemistry and in medicine. The queen of James I., it is said, often sent for his remedies when she or any one of the royal children was ill, and Prince Henry, the eldest son of James I., was so much in sympathy with Raleigh that he said openly that no king but his father "would keep so rare a bird in so ill a cage."

You shall now receive, dear wife, my last words in these my last lines. My love I send you, that you may keep it when I am dead; and my counsel, that you may remember it when I am

no more. I would not by my will present you
with sorrows, dear Bess ; let them go to the grave
and be buried with me in dust. And seeing it is
not the will of God that I shall ever see you more
in this life, bear it patiently and with a heart like
thyself.

Firstly, I send you all the thanks my heart can
conceive, or my words can express, for your many
troubles and cares taken for me ; which, though
they have not taken effect as you wished, yet the
debt is nathless, and pay it I never shall in this
world.

Secondly, I beseech you by the love you bare
me living, do not hide yourself in grief many
days, but seek to help the miserable fortunes of
our poor child. Thy mourning cannot avail me ;
I am but dust. . . . Remember your poor child
for his father's sake, who chose and loved you in
his happiest time. God is my witness it is for
you and *yours* I desired life ; but it is true I disdain myself for begging of it. For know, dear
wife, that your son is the son of a true man, and
one who in his own respect despiseth death, and
all his misshapen grisly forms. I cannot write
much. God knows how hardly I stole the time,
when all sleep ; and it is time to separate my
thoughts from the world. Beg my dead body,

which living is denied thee, and either lay it at
Sherbourne or in Exeter, by my father and
mother. I can write no more. Time and Death
call me away.

The everlasting God, Infinite, Powerful, In-
scrutable; the Almighty God, which is Goodness
itself, Mercy itself; the true light and life, — keep
thee and thine, have mercy on me and teach me
to forgive my persecutors and false witnesses,
and send us to meet again in His Glorious Kingdom. My own true wife, farewell. Bless my
poor boy. Pray for me, and let the good God
fold you both in His arms. Written with the
dying hand of sometime thy husband, but now,
alas! overthrown.

Yours that was, but not now my own,

W. RALEGH.

——◆——

The Same to the Same.

During the last years of Raleigh's captivity the interest
in American discovery was strongly aroused and there
were rumours of rich mines discovered in Guiana. No
man in England knew so much about America as Sir Walter; and the king, as mercenary as he was cowardly, finally
concluded to send Sir Walter on an expedition, although
his sentence was unrevoked and he was still held a prisoner to the crown. He sailed in 1617 for the Orinoco
region, and anchored near some Spanish settlements there.

Almost immediately the old feud broke out, which rankled in the heart of every English sailor whenever the name Spaniard was spoken. The town was attacked and burned, the Spanish governor was killed, and also Raleigh's son Walter, who had gone with him on this expedition. It was upon his return, when he could clearly foresee his doom, that Sir Walter wrote the following to his wife to console her for the death of their son.

MARCH 22, 1618.

SWEET HEART, — I was loath to write, because I knew not how to comfort you ; and God knows I never knew what sorrow meant till now. All that I can say to you is, that you must obey the will and providence of God ; and remember that the Queen's Majesty bare the loss of Prince Henry with a magnanimous heart, and the Lady Harrington of her only son. Comfort your heart, dearest Bess, I shall sorrow for us both ; I shall sorrow the less because I have not long to sorrow, because not long to live. I refer you to Secretary Winhord's letter, who will give you a copy of it if you send for it. Therein you shall know what has passed. I have written but that letter, for my brains are broken, and it is a torment for me to write, and especially of misery. I have desired Mr. Secretary to give my Lord Carew a copy of his letter. . . . You shall hear from me if I live, from the Newfoundland, where I mean to make clean my ships and revictual, for I have tobacco enough to pay for it. The Lord bless and comfort you, that you may bear patiently the death of your valiant son.

Yours,

W. RALEGH.

Raleigh was arrested immediately after landing, and, without any new trial, was condemned to death under the old sentence which for fourteen years had been hanging over his head. His wife, always devoted, made ineffectual efforts to save him. After his execution she wrote her brother, Sir Nicholas Carew : —

"I desire, good brother, that you will be pleased to let me bury the worthy body of my noble husband in your church at Beddington, where I desire to be buried also. They have given me his dead body, though they denied me his life. This night he shall be brought you with two or three of my men. Let me hear presently. God hold me in my wits.

"ELIZABETH RALEGH."

Sir Walter was not buried in Beddington notwithstanding this request. His remains are in St. Margaret's Church just over the way from Westminster Abbey, and his faithful wife is not buried beside him. Her brief letter, with its supplication, "God hold me in my wits," is worth volumes of lamentation.

From Kate, Duchess of Buckingham, to her Husband, George Villiers, Duke of Buckingham.

The following letter was written by KATE VILLIERS, Duchess of Buckingham, to her handsome and profligate husband, when he was absent in Spain, as friend and companion to Prince Charles, afterwards Charles I. It is to this same Duke of Buckingham, familiarly called "Steenie" by James I. and the prince, that King James wrote the letter quoted on page 200.

The negotiations for Charles's marriage with the Infanta, which took the Prince and his suite to Madrid, at the time the following letters were written, were carried on for some time, but the alliance was so obnoxious to the English people that it was finally given up.

That the Duke of Buckingham was very attractive in person, and capable of inspiring most ardent attachments, is proved by the affection the king and prince felt for him as well as by the extravagant terms of his wife's letters.

1623.

MY DEAR LORD, — I humbly thank you that you were pleased to write so many letters to me, which was so great a comfort to me as you cannot imagine, for I protest to God I have had a grievous time of this our grievous parting, for I am sure it has been so to me, and my heart has felt enough more than I hope it ever shall do again; and I pray God release me out of it by your speedy coming hither again to her that doth as dearly love

you as ever woman did man ; and if everybody did
love you but a quarter as well, you were the happiest man that ever was born, but that is impossible. But I protest I think you are the best
beloved that ever favourite was, for all that have
true worth in them cannot but love your sweet
disposition. If I were not so near to you as I
thank God I am, I could say no less, if I said truth,
for I think there never was such a man born as
you are ; and how much am I bound to God that I
must be that happy woman, to enjoy you from all
other women, — I, the unworthiest of all, to have
so great a blessing ! Only this I can say for myself, you could never have had one that could love
you better than your poor, true loving Kate doth,
poor now in your absence, but else the happiest
and richest woman in the world. I thank you for
your long letter ; I think I must give Sir Francis
Cottington thanks for it too, because you say he
bade you write long letters. I am beholden to
him for that, because I am sure he knew they could
never be *too* long for me, for it is all the comfort I
have now to read often over your letters. My
reason that I desired you not to do it was for fear
of troubling you too much ; but, since you think it
none, I am much bound to you for it, and I beseech you to continue it.

I hope you see by this, I have not omitted writing by any that went, for this is the sixteenth letter, at the least, I have written you since you went, whereof two of them I sent by the common post; but I hope they will all come safely to your hands.

I thank you for sending me so good news of our young mistress.[1] I am very glad she is so delicate a creature, and of so sweet a disposition; indeed, my Lady Bristow sent me word she was a very fine lady and as good as fine. I am very glad of it, and that the Prince likes her so well, for the King says he is wonderfully taken with her. That is a wonderful good hearing, for it were a great pity but the Prince should have one he could love, because I think he will make a very honest husband, which is the greatest comfort in this world, to have man and wife love truly.

I told the King of the private message the Infanta sent the Prince, to wear a great ruff; he laughed heartily at it, and said it was a good sign. I am very glad you sent to hasten the ships. I hope you mean not to stay long, which I am very glad of. . . .

I thank God, Moll is very well with her wean-

---

[1] The Infanta of Spain, the proposed wife of Charles I.

ing. Thus, with my daily prayers for our happy meeting, I take my leave.

Your loving and obedient wife,

KATE BUCKINGHAM.

I pray send me word when you come.

The little Moll mentioned above was the daughter of the Duke, of whose baby ways the Duchess gives the following lively description in another of her letters while the Duke is at this time absent.

MOLL is very well, I thank God, and when she is set upon her feet and held by the sleeves, she will not go slowly, but stamp and set one foot afore another very fast, that I think she will run before she can go. She loves dancing extremely, and when the saraband be played, she will get her finger and her thumb together, offering to snap; and then when *Tom Duff* is sung, then will she shake her apron, and when she hears the tune of the clapping dance my Lady Frances Hubert taught the Prince, she will clap both her hands together and on her heart; and she can tell the tunes as well as any of us can, and, as they change the tunes, she will change her dancing. I would you were but here to see her, for you would take much delight in her now she is so full of pretty plays and tricks; and she has gotten

a trick that when they dance her, she will cry
" Ha ! ha ! " and Nicholas will dance with his legs,
and she will imitate him as well as she can. If
one lay her down, she will kick her legs over her
head ; but I hope as she grows older she will grow
more modest. Everybody says she is more like
you than any other. You shall have her picture
very shortly. I am very glad you have the pearls
and that you like them so well ; and I am sure
they do not help you to win the ladies' hearts.
Yourself is a jewel that will win the hearts of *all
the women in the world*, but I am confident it is
not in their power to win *your* heart from a heart
that is, was, and ever shall be yours till death.

KATE.

----◆----

Endymion Porter to his Wife, Olive Porter.

Another companion of Prince Charles on this embassy
to Spain for the wooing of the Infanta, was Mr. Endymion
Porter, who had been, in early life, resident in Spain,
and in later years attached to the family of the great Duke
of Buckingham. He was himself of good family, and is a
most picturesque figure of a cavalier of this age. His
marriage with his wife, Olive, to whom these letters are
addressed, was purely a love-match, and it seems to have
been a very happy one, although somewhat troubled by
Olive's jealousy during his frequent absences, — a jealousy which the free manners of the age and the society in

which he lived made not unreasonable. A great number
of his early letters are devoted to soothing her jealous
alarms and protesting his affection.   In one of his letters
he says : —

"If you did but know how truly I love you, you would
never be jealous of me, and had you such reports of me as
you credited for truths, yet, if you loved me half as well
as I desire, you would not so easily give credit to them."

That he loved Olive one has little doubt, in re-reading his
letters, yet for his fidelity he protests too much ; and when
he writes that the Duke of Buckingham and himself "think
of nothing but our wives," we suspect him of being in
league with the Duke, and of writing for the eye of Kate
Villiers as well as the jealous Olive.

Even the sober Prince Charles seems to have been somewhat infected by absence from home and by the climate
of Spain, and there are authentic reports of a dewy morning's adventure, in which Endymion Porter helped the
prince to clamber a garden wall that he might catch sight
of the Infanta in her early walk in the palace gardens,
and thus have a more undisturbed sight of his intended
bride than the etiquette of the Spanish court afforded.   I
should like to hope that this was the least culpable adventure in which Endymion engaged, but there is some mention (in letters not intended for Olive's eye) of an "angel,"
also referred to as the "mistress of his heart," whom he
seems to have met during this journey abroad, which would
give some colour to Olive's jealousy.

When Endymion's fortunes in later years were clouded
by his devotion to the royal family, his wife dropped all
jealous reproaches and became a most helpful and noble
wife. He went to France with Queen Henrietta Maria,

and Olive Porter, remaining in England, used great address and courage in protecting and preserving his fortunes and interests at home.

No date (probably 1622).

MY DEAREST OLIVE, — Thy care in sending to me shows me how truly thou lovest me, and thy fear of my inconstancy argues no want of affection, only of faith, which, if any good works of mine may strengthen, I will come on my knees to see thee, and put out my eyes rather than look with unchaste desire upon any creature while I breathe ; and to be more secure of me, I would have thee inquire if ever I was false to any *friend*, and then to consider what a traitor I should be, if to a wife (and to such a wife !) so virtuous and good, I should prove false, and not to my friends. Dear Olive, be assured that I strive to make myself happy in nothing but in thee, and therefore I charge you to be merry, and to cherish your health and life, the more because I live in you. But what can I say, or what in the least little can I do? *Love you?* That I do and ever shall, as he who vows never to be anybody's but your true husband.

ENDYMION PORTER.

The Same to the Same.

Written during his absence in Spain with Prince Charles
.   and the Duke of Buckingham.

MADRID, April 17, 1623, N. S.

MY DEAREST OLIVE, — Since my coming into
Spain I have received four letters from you, and
the two first with so much kindness in them that
I thought my love rewarded; but the two last are
so full of mistrust and falsehood that I rather fear
you have changed your affection than that you
have any sure ground for what you accuse me of
in them; for, as I hope for mercy at God's hands,
I neither kissed nor touched any woman since
I left you; and for the inn-keeper's daughter at
Bullen, I was so far from kissing her, *that, as I
hope to be saved, I cannot remember if I saw any such
woman.* No, Olive, I am not a dissembler, for I
assure you the grief I suffered at parting with you
gave me no leave to entertain such base thoughts,
but rather lasted in me like a consumption, in-
creasing daily more and more. But seeing you
have taken a resolution (without hearing what I
could say) '' never to be confident of me again,"
I will procure how to be worthy of your best

thoughts and study how to have patience for any neglect from you.

I understood that you sent me two kisses by a gentleman. God reward you for them; and, since your bounty increases, I think it unfit my thanks should diminish. I perceive you would be glad to hear of my kissing of inn-keepers' daughters every day, that you might have some excuse to do that which nothing but my unworthiness and misfortune can deserve. Alas! sweet Olive, why should you go about to afflict me? Know that I live like a dying man, and one that cannot live long without you. My eyes grow weary in looking upon anything, as wanting that rest they took in the company and the sight of thine, nor can I take pleasure in sports, for there is none that seems not a monster to my understanding where Olive is wanting. With thee I only entertain myself, and were it not for the force of remembering thee, I know not how my life should have maintained itself so long.

You have a great deal of advantage over me in this absence; your two little babes and their affection, they serve to entertain you, and it teaches you to forget me; yet for pity in this banishment and misery, let me hear of your health and theirs, for I assure you it will be no small comfort to

me. Good Olive, let me receive no more quarrelling letters from you, for I desire nothing but your
love, it being the only thing that affords me pleasure in this vile world. Send me word how the
children do, and whether Charles be black or fair,
and who he is like. But I am sure your nurse
will swear that he hath my eyes and nose, and
you may perchance be angry and say *you* never
saw anything so like some brother of yours. I
would to God I could hear the discourse. I would
never come to Bullen to kiss my host's daughter,
although you should entreat me to.

The Prince visited the Infanta yesterday, whose
beauty gave him a just occasion to like her. The
marriage will be I know not when, but if my desires to see you would hasten it I assure you I
would make bold to trouble you before the two
months which you allow me in your last letter.

I have sent my Lady Villiers a tobacco-box. I
hope she will esteem it a token of my love, and
that you will deliver it with the best grace your
father taught you, which was, "Hold up your
head, Olive."

Now I am sure you laugh and think I have forgot the just cause I have to be angry at you, but
till I receive more kisses from you I shall not be
well pleased. I pray you remember my humble

service to my Lady,[1] and tell her that my Lord and I wish you both here very often. We both live very honest, and think of nothing but our wives.

I thought to have sent you a token of some value, but found my purse and my good-will could not agree, and considering my letter would be welcome unto you I leave to do it, only this ring which I hope you will esteem, if not for love, I think for charity. The conceit is, that it seems two, as you turn it, but is only one.

God Almighty bless you, and George, and Charles, and give you his grace, and I pray you remember to pray for him who will ever be

Your true, loving husband,

ENDYMION PORTER.

———◆———

The Winthrop Letters.

One does not look for much sentiment, or any very fervent expression of it, among the Puritan founders of New England; so that when one finds it in the letters or literature of these stern and severe people, it is like finding a flower in the cleft of a rock. JOHN WINTHROP, the first governor of the Massachusetts Bay Colony, was a man cast in a

———

[1] "My Lady" was Kate Buckingham, whose letter to her lord I have before quoted. History does not quite testify to the truth of the avowal that they thought of nothing but their wives.

somewhat tenderer mould than some of his contemporary Puritan brethren, and his letters to his wife Margaret are full of affection, while her replies not only breathe most perfect womanly submission, but are as ardent as the tenderest lover could desire.

I have quoted, as a prefix to some of the letters of John Winthrop and his wife, the following letter from ANNE WINTHROP, his mother, to her husband, which is a very quaint wifely epistle of the sixteenth century.

Anne Winthrop to her Husband.

No date.

I HAVE received (right dear and well-beloved) from you this week a letter, though short, yet very sweet, which gave me a lively taste of those sweet and comfortable words which always, when you be present with me, are wont to flow most abundantly from your loving heart, — whereby I perceive that whether you be present with me or absent from me, you are ever one towards me, and your heart remaineth always with me. Wherefore, laying up this persuasion of you in my breast, I will most assuredly, the Lord assisting me by his grace, bear always the like loving heart unto you again, until such time as I may more fully enjoy your loving presence; but in the meantime I will remain as one having a great inheritance, or rich treasure, and it being by force kept from him, or he being in a strange country and cannot enjoy

it, longeth continually after it, sighing and sor-
rowing that he is so long bereft of it, yet rejoiceth
that he hath so great treasure pertaining to him,
and hopeth that one day the time will come that
he shall enjoy it and have the whole benefit of it.
So I, having a good hope of the time to come, do
more patiently bear the time present, and I pray
send me word if you be in health, and what success you have with your letters.

I sent to Cokynes (?) for the capones, and
they are not yet fat; as soon as they be ready
I will send them. I send you this week, by my
father's man, a shirt and five pair of hose. I
pray sell all these; if ye would any for your own
wearing I have more a-knitting. I pray send me
a pound of starch by my father's man. You may
very well send my Bible if it be ready. Thus,
with my very hearty commendations, I bid you
farewell, committing you to Almighty God, to
whom I commend you in my daily prayers, as I
am sure you do me; the Lord keep us now and
ever. Amen.

Your loving wife,

ANNE WINTHROP.

Je vous rende grace de la bien souvenance que
vous avez de moi Bible François. Je vous prie
de l'envoyer en bréf par le Roullier.

If my brother Winthrop be at London, I pray forget not to say my very hearty commendations unto him.

———◆——

John Winthrop to Margaret Tyndal.

The following letter is from John Winthrop to his betrothed wife Margaret Tyndal shortly before their marriage. She was his third wife, although he was barely thirty at the time of his marriage with her. This is as unique a love-letter as can be found in the annals of courtship, and its mixture of ardent affection with religious devotion, its adaptation of scripture to the language of passionate wooing, is not equalled by anything in literature.

To my best beloved, Mrs. MARGARET TYNDAL, at Great Maplestead, Essex. Grace, mercy, and peace, etc.

My own beloved spouse, my most sweet friend and faithful companion of my pilgrimage, the happy and hopeful supply (next Christ Jesus) of my greatest losses, I wish thee a most plentiful increase of all true comfort in the love of Christ, with a large and prosperous addition of whatsoever happiness the sweet estate of holy wedlock, in the kindest society of a loving husband, may afford thee. Being filled with the joy of thy love, and wanting opportunity of more familiar communion with thee, which my heart

fervently desires, I am constrained to ease the
burthen of my mind by this poor help of my
scribbling pen, being sufficiently assured that,
although my presence is that which thou desirest,
yet in the want thereof these lines shall not be
unfruitful of comfort unto thee. And now, my
sweet love, let me awhile solace myself in the remembrance of our love, of which this springtime
of our acquaintance can put forth as yet no more
but the leaves and blossoms, whilst the fruit lies
wrapped up in the tender bud of hope; a little
more patience will disclose this good fruit, and
bring it to some maturity. Let it be our care and
labour to preserve these hopeful buds from the
beasts of the field, and from frosts and other injuries of the air, lest our fruit fall off ere it be
ripe, or lose aught in the beauty and pleasantness
of it. Let us pluck up such nettles and thorns as
would defraud our plants of their due nourish-
ment; let us prune off superfluous branches; let
us not stick at some labour in watering and ma-
nuring them : the plenty and goodness of our fruit
shall recompense us abundantly. Our trees are
planted in a fruitful soil; the ground and pattern
of our love is no other but that between Christ
and his dear spouse, of whom she speaks as she
finds him. " My well-beloved is mine and I am

his." Love was their banqueting-house, love was their wine, love was their ensign; love was his invitings, love was her faintings; love was his apples, love was her comforts; love was his embracings, love was her refreshing; love made him see her, love made her seek him; love made him wed her, love made her follow him; love made him her saviour, love made her his servant. Love bred our fellowship, let love continue it, and love shall increase it until death dissolve it. . . .

Now, my dear heart, let me parley a little with thee about trifles, for when I am present with thee my speech is prejudiced by thy presence, which draws my mind from itself. I suppose now, upon thy uncle's coming, there will be advising and counselling of all hands; and amongst many I know there will be some that will be provoking thee in these indifferent things, — as matter of apparel, fashions, and other circumstances, rather to give content to their vain minds, savouring too much of the flesh, &c., than to be guided by the rule of God's word, which must be the light and the Rule. . . . I confess that there be some ornaments which, for virgins and knight's daughters, &c., may be comely and tolerable, which yet, in so great a change as thine is, may well admit a change also. I will meddle with no particulars, neither do I think it shall be needful; thine own wisdom and godliness shall teach thee sufficiently what to do in such things, and the good assurance which I have of thy unfeigned love towards me makes me persuaded that thou wilt have care of my contentment, seeing it must be a chief stay to thy comfort; and with all the great and sincere desire which I have that there might be no discouragement to daunt the edge of my affections, while they are truly labouring to settle and repose themselves in thee, makes me thus watchful and jealous of the least occasion that Satan might stir up to our discomfort. He that is faithful in the least will be faithful in the greatest, but I am too fearful I do thee wrong; I know thou wilt not grieve me for trifles. Let me entreat thee (my sweet love) to take all in good part, for it is all of my love to thee, and in my love I shall requite thee. . . .

Lastly, for my farewell (for thou seest my lothness to part with thee makes me tedious), take courage unto thee, and cheer up thy heart in the Lord, for thou knowest that Christ, the best of husbands, can never fail thee: he never dies, so as there can be no grief at parting; he never changes, so as once beloved and ever the same; his ability is ever infinite, so as the dowry and

inheritance of his sons and daughters can never
be diminished. As for me, a poor worm, dust and
ashes, a man full of infirmities, subject to all sins,
changes, and chances which befall the sons of
men, how should I promise thee anything of myself, or, if I should, what credence couldst thou
give thereto, seeing God only is true and every
man a liar? Yet so far as a man may presume
upon some experience, I may tell thee that my
hope is, that such comfort as thou hast already
conceived of my love towards thee shall (through
God's blessing) be happily continued; his grace
shall be sufficient for me, and his power shall be
made perfect in my greatest weakness; only let
thy godly, kind, and sweet carriage towards me
be as fuel to the fire, to minister a constant supply
of meet matter to the confirming and quickening
of my dull affections. This is one end why I write
so much unto thee, that if there should be any
decay in kindness, &c., through my default and
slackness hereafter, thou might have some pat-
terns of our first love by thee, to help the recovery
of such disease. Yet let our trust be wholly in
God, and let us constantly follow him by our
prayers, complaining and moaning unto him of
our poverty, imperfections, and unworthiness, until
his fatherly affection break forth upon us, and he

speak kindly to the hearts of his poor servant and handmaid, for the full assurance of grace and peace through Christ Jesus, to whom I now leave thee (my sweet spouse and only beloved). God send us a safe and comfortable meeting on Monday morning. Farewell. Remember my love and duty to my Lady, thy good mother, with all kind and due salutations to thy uncle E. and all thy brothers and sisters.

Thy husband by promise,

JOHN WINTHROP.

GROTON, where I wish thee, April 4, 1618.

My father and mother salute thee heartily, with my Lady and the rest.

If I had thought my letter would have run to half this length I would have made choice of a larger paper.

———◆———

Margaret Winthrop to her Husband.

The next letter is from Margaret Tyndal, now become Mrs. Winthrop, written in their early wedded life, before her husband had departed for the home in the New World. It is rather more submissive than the more modern ideas of woman's dependence upon man would warrant, but

Margaret Tyndal was probably bred up in Milton's ideas of the relations of the man and woman, " *He* for God only, *she* for God in him."

GROTON, Nov. 22, 1627.

MY MOST SWEET HUSBAND, — How dearly welcome thy kind letter was to me I am not able to express. The sweetness of it did much refresh me. What can be more pleasing to a wife than to hear of the welfare of her best beloved, and how he is pleased with her poor endeavours? I blush to hear myself commended, knowing my own wants. But it is your love that conceives the best, and makes all things seem better than they are. I wish that I may always be pleasing to thee, and that those comforts we have in each other may be daily increased, as far as they be pleasing to God. I will use that speech to thee that Abigail did to David; I will be a servant to wash the feet of my lord. I will do any service wherein I may please my good husband. I confess I cannot do enough for thee; but thou art pleased to accept the will for the deed, and rest contented.

I have many reasons to make me love thee, whereof I will name two: first, because thou lovest God; and secondly, because thou lovest me. If these two were wanting, all the rest would

18

be eclipsed.   But I must leave this discourse, and go about my household affairs.   I am a bad house-wife to be so long from them ; but I must needs borrow a little time to talk with thee, my sweet heart.   The term is more than half done.   I hope thy business draws to an end.   It will be but two or three weeks before I see thee, though they be long ones.   God will bring us together in his good time ; for which I shall pray.   I thank the Lord we are all in good health.   We are very glad to hear so good news of our son Henry.   The Lord make us thankful for all his mercies to us and ours.   And thus, with my mother's and my own best love to yourself and all the rest, I shall leave this scribbling.   The weather being cold makes me make haste.   Farewell, my good husband ; the Lord keep thee.

> Your obedient wife,
> MARGARET WINTHROP.

——◆——

John Winthrop to his Wife.

To my very loving wife, MRS. WINTHROP, at Groton, in Suffolk.

> CHILDERDITCH, Jan. 1, 1623.

MY SWEET SPOUSE, — I praise our good God, and do heartily rejoice in thy welfare and of the rest of our family, longing greatly to be with thee, whom my soul delights in above all earthly things; these times of separation are harsh and grievous while they last, but they shall make our meeting more comfortable. It will be Monday at night before I can come home. In the meantime my heart shall be with thee, as it is always, and as thy love deserves. I am now at Childerditch, from whence I cannot go till Saturday, and it will be too far to come home; so as I intend to keep the Lord's day at Sir Harry Mildmaies.

The news here is of a Parliament, to begin the 12th of February next. The Earl of Oxford came out of the Tower upon Tuesday last. Other things I shall relate to thee when we meet; only I thought good to write lest thou shouldst be troubled at my not coming on Saturday night. Thus commending thee and all ours to the gracious blessing and holy providence of our Heavenly Father, I heartily embrace my sweet wife in the arms of my best affections, ever resting.

Thy faithful husband,

J. WINTHROP.

The Same to the Same.

The following letter was written by John Winthrop after he had parted from his family and embarked on the " Arbella " for Massachusetts. It seems to have been agreed upon between them that they should think of each other at " five of the clock Mondays and Fridays." No lovers could have been more devoted in the first hour of troth-plight than these two who had then been twelve years wedded.

To Mrs. MARGARET WINTHROP, the elder, at Groton.

> From aboard the " Arbella," riding at the COWES, March 28, 1630.

MY FAITHFUL AND DEAR WIFE, — It pleaseth God that thou shouldst once again hear from me before our departure, and I hope this shall come safe to thy hands. I know it will be a great refreshing to thee. And blessed be his mercy, that I can write thee so good news, that we are all in very good health, and, having tried our ship's entertainment now more than a week, we find it agree very well with us. Our boys are well and cheerful, and have no mind of home. They lie both with me, and sleep as soundly in a rug (for we use no sheets here) as ever they did at Groton, and so I do myself, I praise God. The wind hath been against us this week and more ; but this day it is come fair to the north, so as we are preparing, by God's assistance, to set sail in the morning. We have only four ships ready, and some two or three Hollanders go along with us. The rest of our fleet, being seven ships, will not be ready this sennight. We have spent now two Sabbaths on shipboard very comfortably, God be praised, and are daily more and more encouraged to look for the Lord's presence to go along with us. Henry Kingsbury hath a child or two in the " Talbot" sick of the measles, but like to do well. One of my men had them at Hampton, but he was soon well again. We are, in all our eleven ships, about seven hundred persons, passengers, and two hundred and forty cows, and about sixty horses. The ship which went from Plymouth carried about one hundred and forty persons, and the ship which goes from Bristowe carrieth about eighty persons. And now (my sweet soul) I must once again take my last farewell of thee in Old England. It goeth very near to my heart to leave thee ; but I know to whom I have committed thee, even to Him who loves thee much better than any husband can, who hath taken account of the hairs of thy head, and puts all thy tears in his bottle, who can and (if it be for his glory) will bring us together again with peace and comfort. Oh, how it refresheth my heart to think that I shall yet again see thy sweet face in the land of the living! — that lovely countenance, that I have so much delighted in, and beheld with so great content. I have hitherto been so much taken up with business, as I could seldom look back to my former happiness; but now, when I shall be at some leisure, I shall not avoid the remembrance of thee, nor the grief for thy absence. Thou hast thy share with me, but I hope the course we have agreed upon will be some ease to us both. Mondays and Fridays, at five of the clock at night, we shall meet in spirit till we meet in person. Yet, if all these hopes should fail, blessed be our God that we are assured we shall meet one day, if not as husband and wife, yet in a better condition. Let that stay and comfort thy heart. Neither can the sea drown thy husband, nor enemies destroy, nor any adversity deprive thee of thy husband or children. Therefore I will only take thee now and my sweet children in mine arms, and kiss and embrace you all, and so leave you with my God. Farewell, farewell. I bless you all in the name of the Lord Jesus. I salute my daughter Winth., Matt., Nan., and the rest, and all my good neighbours and friends. Pray all for us. Farewell. Commend my blessing to my son John. I cannot now write

to him; but tell him I have committed thee and
thine to him. Labour to draw him yet nearer to
God, and he will be the surer staff of comfort to
thee. I cannot name the rest of my good friends,
but thou canst supply it. I wrote, a week since,
to thee and Mr. Leigh, and divers others.

Thine wheresoever,

Jo. Winthrop.

———◆———

The Sidney Letters.

One of the most interesting families in English history
is the Sidney family, of which two such rare characters
as Philip Sidney, in Elizabeth's reign, and Algernon Sidney, in the reign of Charles I., are scions. The first illustrious member of this house was Sir Henry Sidney, the
father of Philip, a broad-minded and noble-hearted gentleman, a patron of literature and interested in the advance-
ment of all that was good for his country and for mankind.
His sons were the famous Sir Philip Sidney, and Robert, a
younger son, whose son Robert became the second Earl of
Leicester, and the father of Algernon Sidney. This Robert, the second Earl of Leicester, married Dorothy Percy,
the eldest daughter of the Earl of Northumberland. Their
union seems to have been from first to last a profoundly
happy one. The Earl outlived his wife several years, and
in his journal, which he kept regularly, he gives the
following account of her death and her last farewell to
him : —

"On Saturday, the 20th of August, 1659, between six

and seven o'clock in the morning, my wife sent one of her women, who came in some haste, to tell me she desired to speak to me. I was not yet out of bed, but I put on my clothes as fast as I could, and came and kneeled by her bedside, where she had caused herself to be raised, and sat up, being stayed by one of her women. I took her by the hand and kissed it. She inclined her face toward me, and said, 'My dearest heart, I find that I must very quickly leave you, but before I die I desire to say a few words unto you, and many I cannot say. Love God above all; fear him and serve him. My love has been great and constant unto you,' — then she wept gently, — 'and I beseech you pardon my anger, my angry words, my passions, and whatsoever wherein I have offended you, even all my faults and failings towards you. Pray for me in this my weak estate and near approach of death. Commend me to my dear boy. I should have been glad to see him before I die. . . . Keep all your promises, and trouble not yourself for me. I pray God you may live happily when I am gone, and that God will be pleased to take you at that time when he shall find it best for you. Fear God, love God, serve God. Remember me and love my memory. Think continually upon eternity. I can say no more, so, my dear lord, farewell.' Then, inclining her face to mine as well as she could, and gently pressing my hand, she said, 'God bless you, and now lay me down to rise no more.' "

Some of Lady Dorothy's letters to her husband and to her son, Algernon Sidney, are preserved among the papers of the Sidney family. The following, which is written in the sixteenth year of their wedded life, is evidently in answer to a letter in which the Earl has reproved her for complaining that his letters did not reach her promptly.

Lady Dorothy Sidney to her Husband.

PENSHURST, Feb. 7, 1636.

MY DEAREST HEART, — For my exceptions to your silence I humbly ask your pardon, for since I have received three letters from you, — the one by Mr. Auger, who I have not yet seen, but he writes to me with much civility, and I hear that he speaks of you with all the honour, estimation, and affection that can be, which should make him as welcome to me as any of my brothers. Two letters more have I had since his arrival; but that which was first written came last to my hands, for my Lord of Holland sent it to me yesterday, and the other, which was dated the 27th Jan., was received by me the 4th of Feb.

They all brought such contentment to me as nothing but your own person can give me a joy beyond it; and though you reproach me for chiding, yet I hope the consideration of the cause shall free me from any further punishment than the gentle rebuke you have already given me.

By the two letters here enclosed you will find a change from what I heretofore declared to you; and besides the good success which is now expected of your negotiations, I find there is a general applause of your proceedings, which is no small delight to me and I hope will be a great encouragement to you; for though I confess your labours to be very great, yet I trust the conclusion will be very good, and then all the pains will be remembered with pleasure and advantage to you. . . . I hope the three hundred pounds you commanded shall be returned to you at the time appointed, and when more is received it shall be disposed of according to your direction.

The present, also, for the Queen of France I will be very careful to provide; but it cannot be handsome for that proportion of money which you do mention; for those bone laces, if they be good, are dear, and I will send of the best, for the honour of the nation and my own credit.

You persuade my going to London, and there I shall play the ill huswife, which I perceive you are content to suffer rather than I shall remain in this solitariness; and yet my intention is now to remain till the beginning of next month, unless Mr. Auger's going away carry me up sooner. All the children I will leave here, according to your advice; and if you can spare Daniel, I desire that you will send him to me for the time of my being in London.

Mr. Seladine comes in with your letter, whom I am engaged to entertain a little; besides, it is supper-time, or else I should bestow one side of this paper in making love to you; *and since I may with modesty express it, I will say that if it be love to think on you sleeping and waking, to discourse on nothing with pleasure but what concerns you, to wish myself every hour with you, and to pray for you with as much devotion as for my own soul, then certainly it may be said I am in love; and this is all you shall hear at this time from*

Your

Dorothy Leicester.

——◆——

The Earl of Sunderland to Lady Dorothy, his Wife.

The daughter of Lady Dorothy Sidney, who wrote the beautiful letter given above, also named Dorothy, was married to Robert Spenser, Earl of Sunderland. She had been wooed by Edmund Waller in his verses, as the " incomparable Saccharissa," and on the occasion of her marriage with Spenser, the poet wrote her sister, Lady Lucy Sidney, a letter which is famous for its wit and playful irony. In it he says : —

"May my Lady Dorothy, if we may yet call her so, suffer as much, and have the like passion for this young lord whom she has preferred to the rest of mankind, as others have had for her. And may his love, before the year go about, make her taste the first curse imposed on mankind, the pain of becoming a mother. May her first-born be none of her own sex, nor so like her, but that he may resemble her lord as much as herself. May she, that always affected silence and retirement, have the house filled with the noise and number of her children, and here-after of her grandchildren, and then may she arrive at that great curse, so much declined by fair ladies, old age; may she live to be very old, and yet seem young, — be told so by her glass, yet have no aches to inform her of the truth; and when she shall appear to be mortal, may her lord not mourn for her, but go hand in hand with her to that place where we are told there is neither marrying nor giving in marriage, so that, being there divorced, we may all have an equal interest in her again. My revenge being immor-tal, I wish all this may befall her posterity to the world's ends and afterwards.

"EDMUND WALLER."

The happiness of Lady Dorothy and her husband was of brief duration. The Earl of Sunderland was killed in the battle of Newbury, fighting for a cause in which he felt his honour more than his heart was enlisted.

The letter which follows was written at Oxford, then the headquarters of King Charles, four days before the battle in which the Earl met his death.

OXFORD, Sept. 16, 1643.

MY DEAREST HEART, — Since I wrote you last from Sulbey we had some hopes one day to fight with my Lord of Essex's army, we receiving cer-tain intelligence of his being in a field convenient enough, called Riffle field, toward which we ad-

vanced with all possible speed. Upon which he
returned with the body of his army to Tewksbury,
where, by the advantage of the bridge, he was
able to make good his quarter with five hundred
men against twenty thousand. So that though
we were at so near a distance as that we could
have been with him in two hours, his quarter being so strong, it was resolved on Thursday that
we, seeing for the present he would not fight with
us, we should endeavour to force him to it by cut-
ting off his provisions ; for which purpose the best
way was for the body of our army to go back to
Everholme, and for our horse to distress him.
Upon which I and many others resolved to come
for a few days hither, there being no possibility
of fighting very suddenly, where we arrived very
late on Thursday night. As soon as I came I
went to your father's, where I found Allibone,
with whose face I was better pleased than with
any of the ladies here. This expression is so
much a bolder thing than charging my Lord
Essex, that should the letter miscarry, and come
to the knowledge of our dames, I should, by having my eyes scratched out, be cleared of coming
away from the army from fear, where, if I had
stayed, it is odds I should not have lost more
than one.

Last night very good news came to court, that we, yesterday morning, fell upon a horse quarter of the enemy's and cut off a regiment, and that my Lord of Newcastle hath killed and taken prisoners two whole regiment of horse and foot that issued out of Hull, which place he hath great hope to take ere long. By the same messenger last night the King sent the Queen word that he would come hither Monday or Tuesday, upon one of which days, if he alter not his intention, I shall not fail to return to the army. I am afraid our delay before Gloucester has hindered us from making an end of the war this year, which nothing could keep us from doing if we had a month's more time, which we lost there, for we were never in a more prosperous condition; and yet the division does not at all diminish, especially between 142 and 412,[1] by which we receive prejudice. I never saw the King use anybody with greater neglect than 100; and we say he is not used much better by the Queen.

Mrs. Jermyn met my Lord Jermyn, with whom I came, at Woodstock with a coach, who told me she would write to you; which I hope she has done, for since I came here I have seen no crea-

---

[1] These figures are ciphers to denote proper names which it was not politic to write in full.

ture but your father and my uncle, so that I am altogether ignorant of the intrigue of this place. Before I go hence I hope somebody will come from you; however, I shall leave a letter here for you. I have taken the best care I can of my economical affairs. I am afraid I shall not be able to get you a better house, — everybody thinks me mad for speaking about it. Pray bless Poppet[1] for me, and tell her I would have writ to her, but that, upon mature deliberation, I found it to be uncivil to return an answer to a lady in another character [writing] than her own, which I am not yet learned enough to do.

I cannot, by walking my chamber, call to mind anything to set down here, and really I have made you no small compliment in writing you this much, for I have so great a cold that I cannot do anything but sneeze, and mine eyes do nothing but water all the while I am in this posture of hanging down my head.

I beseech you to present his service to my lady, who is most passionately and perfectly *yours,*

SUNDERLAND.

[1] The Earl's little daughter.

Lord and Lady Russell.

The love of Lady RACHEL RUSSELL for her husband, their happy wedded life and her devotion to him unto death, are famous even in the annals of woman's devotion. Guizot in his *L'Amour dans le Mariage* has taken Lady Russell's marriage as a type of the best and finest union, and cites her letters to her husband as a proof that the most romantic sentiment may be preserved in marriage when what is usually considered the age of romance is past.

Before her marriage with Lord Russell (then simply Mr. William Russell) Lady Rachel had been married to Lord Vaughan, and was left, when still young, a widow with large fortune. The estate of Stratton, often referred to in their letters, was Lady Vaughan's own estate, which had become hers through her first marriage. But whatever the advantage of wealth and position on Lady Vaughan's part, the marriage was undoubtedly a love-match on both sides. It would be difficult to find any record of affection more reciprocal, or two hearts more fully at one than these two. After twelve years of wedlock she ends one of her letters thus : " I have nothing new to write you, but I know, as certainly as I live, that I have been for twelve years as passionate a lover as ever woman was, and hope to be so one twelve years more, happy still and entirely yours."

For more than twelve years this perfect union continued without clouds. Lord Russell's great abilities, his patriotism, his unblemished purity of character, gave him a high place in public affairs. He was a devoted servant of King Charles II. but he was also a devoted Protestant, and as such inclined to oppose the succession of James, the Duke of York, fearing that he was too much in sympathy with Catholics for the safety of the government. Through this fear, Russell was drawn into a cabal with five others, — men so differing in their motives and character that they form a group unique enough to be noted here. They were the Duke of Monmouth, the Earl of Essex, Algernon Sidney, Lord Howard, John Hampden (a grandson of the great Hampden of Cromwell's time), and Lord Russell.

The most treasonable among them was Monmouth, a son of Charles II. by Lucy Waters, who aspired to the crown and was beheaded for treason in the following reign of James II. Sidney and Essex were republicans and desired a new form of government; while Russell and Hampden entered into no plots against the crown or the state, but simply advocated a reform of some grievances and wished to make sure that the succession was not Catholic in its tendencies.

As soon as suspicion was aroused against the party, the dastardly Howard turned state's evidence and so escaped all penalty. Monmouth was warned of his danger on account of his relationship to the king, and the Duchess of Monmouth herself went to Charles II. to implore him to spare his son. This he easily promised; but as the Stuart promises were not held at high value, it was thought best that Monmouth should seek safety by flight to the Continent. The event proved his wisdom, for when the conspirators were arrested the Duchess of Monmouth's apartments were the first to be entered and searched. Essex, who was a friend of Russell's, was found with his throat cut in prison shortly after his arrest, and is supposed to have committed suicide. Hampden, strangely enough, was let off with a

19

fine of £40,000; and of the six, only Algernon Sidney and Lord Russell, the two noblest of them all, suffered death on the scaffold.

It was in these last days, when her husband was on trial for his life, that Lady Russell's character showed its most heroic features. Every effort which she could make for his safety and defence she made with a clear-headedness and a calmness which kept all useless emotion under control. When he was put on trial Russell asked the judge: —

"Am I permitted a secretary, my lord, to set down what I shall say ? "

The judge answered, "If any of your servants are present they may act in that office."

"My wife is here," answered Russell, "and will do it." A thrill ran through the whole court as, at the assent of the judge, Lady Russell came quietly forward and took the place beside her husband. She was a daughter of Southampton, who had risked his life in the king's service when the Cromwell party was in power, and had many times filled Charles's empty pockets with supplies of English gold when the young king was in exile and in poverty. Even the sternest royalists were moved to pity by the sight of this daughter of a loyal house, as she sat quietly day after day beside her husband, doing the work of his secretary with an ability that made her indispensable to him. But no efforts, either personal or legal, could save Russell. He himself made some vain appeals and concessions, urged thereto, as he said, not by fear of death, but to satisfy his noble wife, and leave her with the feeling that all possible effort had been made to save him.

When sentence was passed and the day of execution fixed, Lady Russell took leave of him in prison the night before his death. Each of them controlled all emotion that the other might not be grieved or disturbed by the sight of tears or lamentations. When the time came to part, they clasped each other in a long, close embrace, and separated without the utterance of a word or the shedding of a tear. Then Lady Russell went away into her long and lonely widowhood, in which her memories of her husband and her hope of sometime joining him in a blessed future were her chief comforts. One outburst of the heart in one of her letters is most touchingly eloquent. She writes : —

"My heart mourns too sadly, I fear, and *cannot* be comforted, because I have not the dear companion and sharer of my joys and sorrows. I want him to walk with, to talk with, to eat and sleep with. All these things are now irksome to me, the day unwelcome, the night so too ; all company and meals I would avoid if it might be. Yet all this is, that I enjoy not the world in my own way, and this hinders my comfort. When I see my children I remember the pleasure *he* took in them and this makes my heart shrink. Can I regret his quitting a lesser good for a bigger ? Oh, if I *did* steadfastly believe, I could not be so dejected, for I will not injure myself to say, I offer my mind any inferior consolation to supply his loss."

Lady Russell's letters would in no way be remarkable if they were not written so directly from the heart. She speaks sometimes apologetically of her powers as a letter-writer, but the simple feeling with which she writes lends her often an eloquence which is better than that of more famous writers, and the tender domestic atmosphere in which she writes is very beautiful. I add to the following letters by Lady Russell one little note from her husband, written when he was away for a few days on business, which expresses a tenderness as ardent as her letters reveal for him.

It will be noticed that Lady Russell's early letters to her husband are signed "R. Vaughan." She retained this signature till her husband gained his title, and thenceforth signed herself "Russell."

Lord Russell to Lady Russell, written ten Years after Marriage.

BASING, Feb. 8, 1679.

I AM stole from a great many gentlemen in the drawing-room at Basing for a moment, to tell my dearest I have thought of her being here the last time, and wished for her a thousand times; but in vain, alas, for I am just going now to Stratton and want the chariot, and my dearest dear in it. I hope to be with you on Saturday. We have had a very troublesome journey of it, and insignificant enough by the fairness and excess of civility of somebody, but more of that when I see you. I long for that time, and am, more than you can imagine, Your

RUSSELL.

———◆———

Lady Russell to Lord Russell.

TICHFIELD, Aug. 22, 1675.

I WRITE this to my dear Mr. Russell, because I love to be busied in either speaking of him or to him, but the pretence I take is lest the letter

I wrote yesterday should miscarry; so this may again inform you at London, that your coach shall be at Harford Bridge (if God permit) upon Thursday, to wait your coming, and on Saturday I hope to be at Stratton and my sister also. This day she resolved it, so her coach will bring us all. . . . It is an inexpressible joy to consider I shall see the person in the world I most and only long to be with, before another week is past. I should condemn my sense of this happiness as weak and pitiful if I could tell it to you. No, my best life, I can *say* little, but think all you can, and you cannot think too much. My heart makes it all good. I perfectly know my infinite obligations to Mr. Russell, and in it is the delight of her life, who is as much yours as you desire she should be.

RACHEL VAUGHAN.

———◆———

The Same to the Same.

LONDON, Sept. 6, 1680.

MY girls and I being just risen from dinner, Miss Rachel followed me into my chamber, and seeing me take pen and ink asked me what I was going to do. I told her I was going to write to her papa. "So will I," said she, "and while you write I will think what I have to say," and truly, before I could write one word, she came and told me she had done. So I set down her words, and she is hard at the business, as I am not, one would conclude, by the pertinence of this beginning, but my dear man has taken me for better or worse in all conditions, and knows my soul to him. So expressions are but a pleasure to myself, not to him who believes better things of me than my ill rhetoric will induce him to by my words.

To this minute I am not one jot wiser as to intelligence (whatever other improvements my study has made me), but I hope this afternoon's conversation will better me that way. Lady Shaftesbury sends me word if her lord continues as well as he was this morning I shall see her, and my sister was visiting there yesterday. I shall suck the honey from them all, if they be communicative. . . .

Later. I have stayed till Mr. Cheke came in, and he helps me to nothing but a few half-crowns, I expect, at backgammon. Unless I let him read my letter he vows he would tell me no news, if he knew any, and doubting this is not worth his perusal I hasten to shut it up. Lord Shaftesbury was alone, so his lady came not. Your birds came safe to feed us to-morrow.

I am yours, my dear love,

R. RUSSELL.

The Same to the Same.

Stratton, Sept. 30, 1681.

To see anybody preparing and taking their way to see what I long to do a thousand times more than they, makes me not endure to suffer their going without saying something to my best life, though it is a kind of anticipating my joy when we shall meet, to allow myself so much before that time; but I confess I feel a great deal that although I left London with great reluctance (as it is easy to persuade men that a woman does), yet I am not like to leave Stratton with greater.

They will tell you how well I got hither, and how well I found our dear treasure here. Your boy will please you; you will, I think, find him improved, though I tell you so beforehand. They fancy he wanted you, for, as soon as I alighted, he followed, calling " Papa ; " but I suppose it is the word he has most command of, so was not disobliged by the little fellow. The girls were fine in remembrance of the happy 29th of Sept. [Lord Russell's birthday], and we drank your health after a red-deer pie, and at night your girls and I supped on a sack-posset; nay, Master [their son] would have his share, and for haste burnt his fingers in the posset, but he does but rub his hands for it.

It is the most glorious weather that ever was seen. The coach shall meet you at the cabbage-garden; it will be there by eight or a little after, although I hardly guess you will be there so soon, day breaks so late, and indeed the mornings are so misty it is not wholesome to be in the air so early. I do propose going to my neighbour Worsley to-day.

I would fain be telling my dear heart more things, — anything to be in a kind of talk with him, — but I believe Spenser stays for me to despatch this; he was willing to go early, but this writing to you was to be the delight of this morning and the support of the day. It is performed in bed, thy pillow at my back, where thy dear head shall lie, I hope, to-morrow night, and many more, I trust in his mercy, notwithstanding all our enemies or evil-wishers. Love, and be willing to be loved by, thy

R. Russell.

The Duke of Marlborough to the Duchess.

The greatest military leader of England in the eighteenth century, John Churchill, Duke of Marlborough, was under the domination of a ruler more powerful than he. For years the Duchess of Marlborough, imperious, brilliant, ambitious, was the most powerful person in England, ruling even the queen by the ascendancy she had gained through their long friendship.

It is difficult to see now how she held such power, with so little that seems attractive, and with nothing that is amiable, in her character; but that she must have been in youth a woman capable of attaching others to her with hooks of steel is incontrovertible. Marlborough married her for love, and loved her absolutely. His affection breaks through all his letters to her. He writes, " I am heart and soul yours," " I can have no happiness till I am with you;" and his fear of her displeasure or tempers comes in such plaintive bursts as " I am never so happy as when I think you are kind." His motive of life was to please her, and his ambition to conquer all fields that were before him, that he might settle down at home with " the blessing of living quietly with her my soul longs for."

Perhaps fortunately for this much-wished-for peace, the Duke died long before the Duchess, who lived to great old age ; a virago whose last days remind us not a little of those of the Countess of Shrewsbury,[1] in Elizabeth's reign, who spent her last days not only at variance with those about her, but even with her nearest of kin, and who died execrated by those to whom she should have been an object of reverence and love.

HAGUE, April 23, 1706.

I AM very uneasy at not having heard from you since my being in this country ; and, the wind continuing in the east, I am afraid I shall not have the satisfaction of receiving any letter from my

---

[1] See letters to Countess of Shrewsbury, p. 242.

dearest soul before I leave this place, which will
be the next week.   I am yet in uncertainty where
I shall serve this summer, for Cadogan is not yet
returned from Hanover; but by a letter I have
received from the King of Denmark, and that
I send by this post to Lord Treasurer, I see that I
must not depend upon any of the Danish troops;
so that if Hanover should persist in doing the
same, though these people should consent to what
I propose, it will not be in our power to find the
troops necessary, which gives me, as you may
imagine, a good deal of vexation.   I hope my
next will let you know the certainty of what I
shall be able to do.

My dearest soul, my desire of being with you
is so great that I am not able to express the impatience I am in to have this campaign over.   I
pray God it may be so happy that there may be
no more occasion of my coming, but that I may
ever stay with you, my dearest soul.

———◆———

*The Same to the Same, written just after the Battle
of Ramillies.*

RAMILLIES, Monday, May 24, 11 o'clock, 1706.

I DID not tell my dearest soul the design I had
of engaging the enemy, if possible, to a battle,

fearing the concern she has for me might make her uneasy; but I can now give her the satisfaction of letting her know that on Sunday last we fought, and that God Almighty has been pleased to give us a victory. I must leave the particulars to this bearer, Colonel Richards, for, having been on horseback all Sunday, and after the battle marching all night, my head aches to that degree that it is very uneasy to me to write. Poor Bingfield, holding my stirrup for me and helping me on horseback, was killed. I am told that he leaves his wife and mother in a poor condition. I can't write to any of my children, so you will let them know I am well, and that I desire they will thank God for preserving me. And pray give my duty to the Queen, and let her know the truth of my heart, that the greatest pleasure I have in this success is, that it may be a great service to her affairs; for I am sincerely sensible of all her goodness to me and mine. Pray believe me when I assure you that I love you more than I can express.

The Letters of Mr. and Mrs. John Adams.

Especially interesting to Americans are the letters of
John Adams and his wife, which were written when the
American conflict began which made the United States
a nation, and in the course of which correspondence we
may trace many of the events that attended the formation
of the young nation. Mrs. Adams's letters have been
deservedly famous among her countrywomen. They are
homely, sensible, and not without the eloquence of the
heart. She was a tower of strength to her husband, and
deserved the name of Portia he seems to have given her,
and which she often signs herself in writing to him. Like
Brutus's Portia, she was well fathered and well husbanded,
and has much of the stuff of the Roman matron in her
composition. The letters of the pair breathe little of the
romance of passion, but they are among the best specimens
of letters which spring from a union based on harmony of
opinion and highest esteem for each other's virtues, — a
union of real friendship as well as of love, — and most of
their letters appropriately begin, "*My dearest friend.*"

John Adams to his Wife.

PHILADELPHIA, 22 May, 1776.

WHEN a man is seated in the midst of forty
people, some of whom are talking and others
whispering, it is not easy to think what is proper
to write. I shall send you the newspapers, which
will inform you of public affairs and the particular
bickerings of parties in this colony. I am happy

to learn from your letter that a flame is at last raised among the people for the fortification of the harbour. Whether Nantasket or Point Alderton would be proper posts to be taken, I can't say. But I would fortify every place which is proper, and which cannon could be obtained for. Generals Gates and Mifflin are now here. General Washington will be here to-morrow, when we shall consult and deliberate concerning the operations of the ensuing campaign.

We have dismal accounts from Europe of the preparations against us. This summer will be very important to us. We shall have a severe trial of our patience, fortitude, and perseverance. But I hope we shall do valiantly and tread down our enemies.

I have some thoughts of petitioning the General Court for leave to bring my family here. I am a lonely, forlorn creature here. It used to be some comfort to me that I had a servant and some horses. They composed a sort of family for me. But now there is not one creature here that I seem to have any kind of relation to. It is a cruel reflection, which very often comes across me, that I should be separated so far from those babes whose education and welfare lie so near my heart. But greater misfortunes than these must not divert us from superior duties.

Your sentiments of the duties we owe to our country are such as become the best of women and the best of men. Among all the disappointments and perplexities which have fallen to my share in life, nothing has contributed so much to support my mind as the choice blessing of a wife, whose capacity enabled her to comprehend, and whose pure virtue obliged her to approve, the views of her husband. This has been the cheering consolation of my heart in my most solitary, gloomy, and disconsolate hours. In this remote situation I am deprived in a great measure of this comfort. Yet I read and read again your charming letters, and they serve me, in some faint degree, as a substitute for the company and conversation of the writer. I want to take a walk with you in the garden, to go over to the common, the plain, the meadow. I want to take Charles in one hand and Tom in the other, and walk with you, Abby on your right hand and John upon my left, to view the cornfields, the orchards, &c.

Alas, poor imagination! how faintly and imperfectly do you supply the want of originality and reality. But instead of these pleasing scenes of domestic life, I hope you will not be disturbed with the alarms of war. I hope, yet I fear.

Mrs. Adams to her Husband.

23 DECEMBER, 1782.

MY DEAREST FRIEND, — I have omitted writing by the last opportunity to Holland, because I had but small faith in the designs of the owners or passengers, and I had just written so largely by a vessel bound to France, that I had nothing new to say. There are few occurrences in this northern climate at this season of the year to divert or entertain you, and in the domestic way should I draw you the picture of my heart it would be what I hope you would still love though it contained nothing new. The early possession you obtained there, and the absolute power you have obtained over it, leaves not the smallest space unoccupied. I look back to the early days of our acquaintance and friendship as to the days of love and innocence, and, with an indescribable pleasure, I have seen near a score of years roll over our heads with an affection heightened and improved by time, nor have the dreary years of absence in the smallest degree effaced from my mind the image of the dear untitled man to whom I gave my heart. I cannot sometimes refrain considering the honours with which he is invested as badges of my unhappiness. The unbounded

confidence I have in your attachment to me and
to the dear pledges of our affection, has soothed
the solitary hours and rendered your absence more
supportable, for had I loved you with the same ·
affection, it must have been misery to have
doubted. Yet a cruel world too often injures my
feelings by wondering how a person, possessed of
domestic attachments, can sacrifice them by ab-
senting himself for years.

"If you had known," said a person to me the
other day, "that Mr. Adams would have remained so long abroad, would you have consented
that he should have gone?" I recollected myself
a moment, and then spoke the real dictates of my
heart. "If I had known, sir, that Mr. Adams
could have effected what he has done, I would
not only have submitted to the absence I have
endured, painful as it has been, but I would not
have opposed it even though three years more
should be added to the number (which Heaven
avert). I feel a pleasure in being able to sacrifice my selfish passions to the general good, and
in imitating the example which has taught me to
consider myself and family but as the small dust
in the balance when compared with the great
community."

It is now, my dear friend, a long, long time

since I have had a line from you. The fate o῝
Gibraltar leads me to fear that a peace is far
distant, and that I shall see you — God only
knows when. I shall say little about my former
request; not that my desire is less, but, before
this can reach you, 't is probable I may receive
your opinion: if in favour of my coming to you,
I shall have no occasion to urge it further; if
against it, I will not embarrass you by again requesting it. I will endeavour to sit down and
consider it as the portion allotted to me.

Adieu, my dear friend. Why is it that I hear so
seldom from my dear John? But one letter have
I ever received from him since he arrived in
Petersburg. I wrote him by the last opportunity.
Ever remember me, as I do you, with all the tenderness which it is possible for one object to feel
for another, which no time can obliterate, no
distance alter, but which is always the same in the
bosom of

PORTIA.

———◆———

Letter of Warren Hastings to his Wife.

To those who have been interested in the history of
Warren Hastings as Governor-General of India, this letter
to his wife will be doubly interesting as showing the man
more intimately than we can find him in any record of his

20

public life, as we see it through the mist of accusation and defence that arises from his famous trial, made more famous by the triple eloquence of Burke, Fox, and Sheridan, all directed against him.

Hastings's life with his wife, who was always his "beloved Marian," was a peculiarly happy one, and their union more perfect than is usual in a world whose best harmony is likely to be full of discords. Their married life was preceded by what is called, in novels and plays, "a romance." When Hastings left England for India, to take his place as member of the council at Madras, he found, as fellow-passengers on board his ship, a Baron Imhoff and his wife, also on their way to India. Imhoff was a German portrait-painter in needy circumstances, who hoped to find patronage and money at Madras. No evidence is other than that he was a base fellow unworthy of respect and loyalty. That Madame Imhoff was worthy of a good man's affection is proved by the after devotion and life-long love she won from such a man as Hastings. The disparity between the married pair and the unhappiness of the wife were apparent. Hastings became interested in Madame Imhoff, and finally, after he had been ill during the voyage and had recovered under her tender nursing, he found himself deeply in love with her. Perfect frankness seems to have prevailed between himself and Imhoff, and an arrangement was made between them that the unvalued wife should apply for a divorce in a German court, and on receiving her freedom should become the wife of Hastings. The application for divorce was made, Imhoff favouring it; after five years of waiting and litigation the marriage was annulled ; Madame Imhoff was free. Hastings at once married her, and the Baron left India a much richer man than he could have hoped to become by portrait-painting.

Mrs Hastings had two children by her first marriage, whom Hastings adopted, and who seem to have loved him as a father. On his death, at an advanced age, the Baroness Charles Imhoff, wife of one of his adopted children, attended him like a daughter and mourned his loss as if she had lost a parent by tie of blood rather than adoption. In every way the marriage formed with the neglected and misprized wife of Imhoff was fruitful of happiness to all concerned. The letter following was written to Mrs. Hastings after she had left him to go to England in 1784, where he joined her a year later, to enter upon the anxieties of a trial which clouded him for many years with obloquy from which he emerged so completely that the House which impeached him, and from whose decision he appealed to the Lords, rose uncovered to receive him when he appeared before them, twenty years after their decision had been given against him.

———◆———

Warren Hastings to his Wife.

BENARES, Oct. 1, 1784.

MY DEAREST MARIAN, — I am indeed a fortunate man, and am tempted to adopt the term even to superstition ; and no wonder, for the belief has seized others long since, and universally. Last night, at about nine o'clock, Major Sands brought me the news of Pipps's arrival at Calcutta, and (may God bless them both for it!) a short but blessed letter from you, dated the 15th of May, the day of your departure from St.

Helena, and written on board the " Atlas." It tells me only that you were safe on board and well, but it tells enough, and it is written in the language of cheerfulness and of affection. . . .

All my past doubts and the fixed gloom which has so long overspread my imagination are dissipated, like the darkness before the equinoctial sun rising on the plains of Suckrowl (do, my dear Marian, allow me to talk nonsense), and have given place to the confident hope that every dreaded obstruction will follow them, and that I am once more destined to happiness. I am already happy; for, as God is my witness that I prefer your happiness to my own, I feel the measure of my present joy full, with the information that I have recently received. . . .

At what a time will you have arrived in England! If nothing has happened between the " Surprise's " departure and your landing to change the public opinion of your husband (and I think it not likely that it should have been changed), you will find his name standing in high and universal credit; and what a welcome will it be to you! I have now but one wish remaining (yes, one more), viz., to be able to leave the stage of active life while my fortune is in the zenith of its prosperity, and while I have a constitution yet repairable.

I must repress myself, for if I write all that the fulness of my heart is ready to dictate, I shall never come to an end, and I have this to copy. How it is to go I know not. I shall trust one to Mr. Boddam, and the other to Mr. Hay in Calcutta, to be despatched as each shall find means. Adieu, my beloved, my most deserving and lovely Marian. May the God whose goodness I have so wonderfully experienced bless you with health, safety, and comfort, and me with the repossession of my sweet Marian! Amen! Amen! Amen! I never loved you so much as I do at this instant, and as I have loved you since the delightful news of last night. . . .

Adieu, my most beloved, adieu!

Letters of Aaron and Theodosia Burr.

A truly amiable and interesting side of AARON BURR's character is that which we find when we look at his domestic relations with his wife, Theodosia. All the misfortunes of his life came after he was bereft of the loving and intellectual woman who gave purpose and balance to that gifted but erratic nature.

He met his wife, Theodosia Prevost, when he was a young officer in the Revolutionary army. She was a widow with two children, and was ten years Burr's senior. The only hesitation about the marriage was the disparity in

years. But Mrs. Burr was a beautiful and charming woman, then thirty-two or thirty-three. Burr was a man of
intellect developed far beyond his years. He was an im-
petuous lover, and married her in spite of reason. The
marriage turned out most happily, and Mrs. Prevost proved
a wife lovable enough to retain till the last the heart she
had won, which was faithful only to her. He said of her,
" She was the only *perfect lady* I ever knew." High praise
from a man so fastidious ! And he writes to her in one of
his latest letters, after they had been nearly twelve years
wedded : " *It was a knowledge of your mind which first inspired
me with a respect for that of your sex, and with some regret, I
confess, that the ideas which you have often heard me express in
favour of female intellectual powers are founded on what I have
imagined more than on what I have seen, except in you.*"

The letters of Mrs. Burr to her husband are full of sentiment. Her husband's are no less affectionate, and when
he is away from her his letters are full of longings for the
time when he shall return. He seems to have been equally
devoted to their daughter, Theodosia, and writes to her
with fatherly care and tenderness blended with most
charming humour.

Mrs. Burr to her Husband.

New York, Saturday, April, 1785.

I persuade myself this is the last day you
spend in Philadelphia ; that to-morrow's stage
will bring you to Elizabethtown ; that Tuesday
morning you will breakfast with those who pass
tedious hours in regretting your absence and
counting the time till your return. Even little

Theo gives up her place on mamma's lap, to tell dear papa " *come home.*" Tell Augustine he does not know how much he owes me. 'T is a sacrifice I would not make to any human being but himself, nor even to him again. It is the last time in my life I submit to your absence, except from the calls of your profession. All is well at home: Ireson gone on his intended journey; the boys very attentive and industrious; not a loud word spoken by the servants. All in silent expectation await the return of the much-loved lord, but *all faintly* when compared to thy

THEO.

The Same to the Same.

NEW YORK, May, 1785.

I AM vexed that I did not inquire your route more particularly. I cannot follow you in imagination, nor find your spirit when at rest; nor dare I count the hours till your return. They are still too numerous, and add to my impatience. I expect my reward in the health you will acquire. If it should prove otherwise, how I shall hate my acquiescence to your departure. I anticipate good or evil as my spirits rise or fall, but I know no medium; my mind cannot reach that stage of indifference. I fancy all my actions directed by you; this tends to spur my industry and give calm to my leisure.

The family as you left it. Barton never quits the office, and is perfectly obliging. Your dear little daughter seeks you twenty times a day; calls you to your meals, and will not suffer your chair to be filled by any of the family. Judge Hobart called yesterday; says you are absent for a month. I do not admit that among possibilities, therefore am not alarmed. I feel obliged to Mr. Wickham for his delay, though I dare not give scope to my pen; my heart dictates too freely. O my Aaron, how many tender, grateful things rush to my mind at this moment; how much fortitude do I summon to suppress them! You will do justice to my silence, to the inexpressible affection of your *plus tendre amie,*

THEODOSIA.

———◆———

Aaron Burr to his Wife.

ALBANY, 2 Nov., 1785.

I HAVE lived these three days upon the letters I expected this evening, and behold the stage without a line from you. I have been through the rain and dark and mud, hunting up every passenger to catechise them for letters, and can scarce yet believe I am so totally forgotten.

Our trial, of which I wrote you Sunday, goes on moderately. It will certainly last till twelve o'clock Saturday night; longer it cannot, that being the last hour of court. Of course I leave this place on Sunday. Shall be detained at Westchester till about Thursday noon, and be home on Friday. This is my present prospect. A gloomy one, I confess, rendered more so by your unpardonable silence. I have a thousand questions to ask, but why ask of the dumb?

I am quite recovered. The trial in which I am engaged is a fatiguing one, in some respects vexatious. But it puts me in better humour to reflect that you have just received *my* letter of Sunday, and are saying and thinking some good-natured things of me, determining to write anything that can amuse or interest me, everything that can atone for the late silence or compensate for the hard fate that divides us.

Since being here I have resolved that in future you accompany me on such excursions, and I am provoked that I yielded to your idle fears on this occasion. I have told here frequently, within a day or two, that I was never so long from home before, till upon counting the days I find I have been frequently longer. I am so constantly anticipating the duration of this absence, that when I speak of it I realize the whole of it.

Let me find that you have done justice to yourself and me. I shall forgive none, the smallest omission on that head. Do not write by the Monday stage, or, rather, do not send the letter you write, as it is possible I shall leave the stage road in my way to Bedford.

Affectionately adieu,

A. BURR.

The Same to the Same.

This is among the later letters of Burr to his wife, who was then in failing health. She died the following year, after twelve years of happy wedded life.

PHILADELPHIA, 15 Feb., 1793.

I RECEIVED with joy and astonishment, on entering the Senate this minute, your two elegant and affectionate letters. The mail closes in a few minutes, and will scarce allow me to acknowledge your goodness. The roads and ferries have been for some days almost impassable, so that till now no post has arrived since Monday.

It was a knowledge of your mind which first inspired me with a respect for that of your sex, and with some regret, I confess, that the ideas which you have often heard me express in favour of female intellectual powers are founded on what I have imagined more than on what I have seen, *except in you.* I have endeavoured to trace the causes of this rare display of genius in women, and find them in the errors of education, of prejudice, and of habit. I admit that men are equally, nay more, much more to blame than women. Boys and girls are generally educated much in the same way till they are eight or nine years of age, and it is admitted the girls make at least equal progress with the boys; generally, indeed, they make better. Why, then, has it never been thought worth the attempt to discover, by fair experiment, the particular age at which the male superiority becomes so evident? But this is not in answer to your letter; neither is it possible now to answer it. Some parts of it I shall never answer. . . . Your plan and embellishment of my mode of life are fanciful, are flattering and inviting; we will endeavour to realize some of it. Pray continue to write, if you can do so with impunity. I bless Sir J., who, with the assistance of Heaven, has thus far restored you.

In the course of this scrawl I have been several times called to vote, and must apologize to you for its incoherence. Adieu.

A. BURR.

Lord Nelson and Lady Hamilton.

The love of LORD NELSON for Lady Hamilton is so insep-
arable a part of his history that it has become an episode
in English history as well. There are few characters in
the naval annals of England that excite such personal
sympathy and interest as Lord Nelson. The enthusiasm
which was felt for him by every sailor under his command
communicates itself to all who read his life. He was a
man perfectly brave, yet tender to excess; his men said
of him that " he was brave as a lion yet as gentle as a lamb."
His feelings were so acute that when any harsh discipline
was enforced on board his ship he suffered from it as much
as if he had been a woman. Such a nature as this was
likely to be strongly swayed by the passion which seized
him in the prime of manhood, at the height of his fame.
That his love for Lady Hamilton was most genuine and
sincere, no one can doubt. It was so sweeping and absolute that nothing in his life could stand against it. He felt
it a part of his life, his loyalty, and his religion.

The career of Lady Hamilton is one of the most excep-
tional in all the accounts of women of strange and adven-
turous fortunes. Whatever had been her history before
her meeting with Nelson, her devotion to him seems as
sincere and absolute as his for her. She was faithful to
her affection from first to last, and remained faithful to
his memory after death.

That she was a person of almost irresistible charm, we
have overwhelming testimony. Even Southey, who touches
lightly on her history, says, " She was a woman whose personal attractions have scarcely been equalled, and whose
powers of mind were not less fascinating than her person."

At the court of Naples she had carried all hearts before her. The queen, who was a sister of Marie- Antoinette, wrote to her as her dearest friend.

It was at Naples that Nelson first met her, and his affection, begun then, ceased only with his death at the battle of Trafalgar. She was to him "his saint," "his guardian angel." When he was dead they found her picture on his heart. He regarded her with a reverence almost superstitious. When he had his ship cleared for action on the morning of his last battle, and the pictures of Lady Hamilton and his daughter Horatia were taken from the walls of his cabin, where they always hung. he told his men to "take care of his guardian angel." Almost his last words were, "Take care of Lady Hamilton." "I leave Lady Hamilton and my daughter to my country." The yearning of the tender-hearted hero for affection burst out in his last words to Captain Hardy, — "Kiss me, Hardy;" and he died, as he had promised Lady Hamilton, with the last sigh upon his lips for her felicity.

It seems as if England should have regarded his request to "take care of Lady Hamilton." Not only his country, but his brother, who inherited his title, ignored his will and refused to acknowledge any claims. The estate of Merton, where Lady Hamilton had resided during Nelson's absences from home, was loaded with debts, which she made vain efforts to have cleared off, so as to preserve it. She was arrested for debt, actually imprisoned, and finally left England to live in France, in a little town near the sea-coast. Here, one day, an English lady, Mrs. Hunter, was buying some meat at the butcher's for her pet dog, when the shopman said to her, "My lady is English, and there is another lady in town, English too, who would be glad of the meat you buy for your little dog."

Mrs. Hunter, shocked at what she heard, went to seek this English lady. It was Lady Hamilton, then in a dying condition. Mrs. Hunter succoured her and ministered to her, and soon saw her breathe her last.

The letters of Nelson are very numerous, and are written on every occasion on which a letter could be transmitted. When there was danger that they would be opened they are more guarded than those sent by private means, but all breathe most absolute devotion and confidence. The following is written just before his return from sea in 1801, before the death of Sir William Hamilton.

Lord Nelson to Lady Hamilton.

St. George, Kioge Bay, Apr. 25, 1801.

My dearest Friend, — Sir Hyde has just sent me word that the sloop "Arrow" sails for England this day, and I have only time to say that I hope in a fortnight to be in London. I am in expectation every moment of the removal of the fleet from the Baltic. Be that as it may, I will not remain; no, not if I were sure of being made a duke with fifty thousand pounds a year. I wish for happiness to be my reward, not titles or money.

To-morrow is the birthday of Saint Emma. She is my guardian angel. It is not in my power to do much honour to her in this place, but I have invited all the admirals and all the captains who have the happiness of knowing you, and, of course, of experiencing your kindness while in the Mediterranean. You may rely that my saint is more adored in this fleet than all the saints in the Roman Calendar. I know you prayed for me at the Nile and here, and if the prayers of the good, as we are taught to believe, are of avail at the Throne of Grace, why may not yours have saved my life? I own myself a believer in God; and if I have any merit in not fearing death, it is because I feel his power can shelter me when he pleases, and that I must fall when it is his good pleasure.

May the God of heaven and earth bless and preserve you, my dearest friend, for the greatest happiness you can wish for in this world, is the constant prayer of your real, sincere, affectionate friend till death,

NELSON & BRONTÉ.

————◆————

The Same to the Same.

AT SEA, Aug. 21, 1803.

WE have had, my dearest Emma, two days pretty strong gales. The "Canopus" has lost her fore-yard, but we shall put her in order again. This is the fourth gale we have had since July 6, but the "Victory" is so easy at sea that I trust we shall never receive any material damage.

It is never my intention, if I can help it, to go

into any port; my business is at sea, and to get hold of the French fleet; and so I shall, by patience and perseverance. . . .

I entreat that you will let nothing fret you only believe, once for all, that I am ever your own Nelson. I have not a thought, except on you and the French fleet. All my thoughts, plans, and toils tend to those two objects, and I will embrace them both so close, when I can lay hold of either one or the other, that the Devil himself should not separate us. Don't laugh at my putting the French fleet and you together, but you cannot be separated. I long to see you both in your proper places, — the French fleet at sea, you at dear Merton, which, in every sense of the word, I expect to find a paradise. I send you a copy of Gibb's letter, my answer, and a letter to Mr. Noble about your things, and I will take all care that they shall get home safe.

Ever yours

NELSON.

———◆———

The Same to the Same.

This, Nelson's last letter to Lady Hamilton, was found on his desk after death. It is now in the British Museum, and is indorsed with these words in Lady Hamilton's handwriting: " This letter was found open on *his* desk and brought to Lady Hamilton by Captain Hardy. Oh miserable wretched Emma! Oh glorious and happy Nelson!" This letter also enclosed a brief one for his daughter, Horatia.

"VICTORY," Oct. 19, 1805, Noon.
CADIZ, E. S. E. 16 leagues.

My dearest beloved Emma, the dear friend of my bosom. The signal has been made that the enemy's combined fleet are coming out of port. We have very little wind, so that I have no hopes of seeing them before to-morrow. May the God of battles crown my endeavours with success; at all events I will take care that my name shall ever be most dear to you and to Horatia, both of whom I love as much as my own life. And as my last writing before the battle will be to you, so I hope in God that I shall live to finish my letter after the battle. May Heaven bless you, prays

Your

NELSON & BRONTÉ.

Oct. 20. In the morning we were close to the mouth of the straits, but the wind had not come far enough to the westward to allow the combined fleets to weather the shoals of Trafalgar; but they were counted as far as forty sail of

21

ships of war, which I suppose to be thirty-four of the line and six frigates. A group of them was seen off the light-house at Cadiz this morning ; but it blows so very fresh and thick weather that I rather believe they will go into harbour before night. May God Almighty give us success over these fellows and enable us to get a peace.

University Press: John Wilson & Son, Cambridge.

SD - #0011 - 090221 - C0 - 229/152/19 - PB - 9780243029969